YOU'RE GONNA LOVE THIS COLLEGE GUIDE

MARTY NEMKO, Ph.D.

Illustrated by Deborah Zemke

BARRON'S

All inquiries should be addressed to:
Barron's Educational Series, Inc.
250 Wireless Boulevard
Hauppauge, New York 11788
http://www.barronseduc.com

Library of Congress Catalog Card No.: 98-54148
International Standard Book No.: 0-7641-0816-6

Library of Congress Cataloging-in-Publication Data
Nemko, Marty
    You're gonna love this college guide / Marty Nemko ; illustrated
by Deborah Zemke.
        p.   cm.
    Includes index.
    ISBN 0-7641-0816-6 (pbk.)
    1. College choice—United States. 2. College student orientation—
    United States. I. Title.
LB2350.5.N467 1999
378.1'61—dc21   98-54148
                                                                   CIP

PRINTED IN THE UNITED STATES OF AMERICA

98765

Contents

Chapter 3   41
HOW TO GET INTO KILLER COLLEGES WITHOUT KILLING YOURSELF

Chapter 4
FINDING THE MONEY

Chapter 5
THE KEYS TO A GREAT COLLEGE EXPERIENCE

ACKNOWLEDGMENTS

Before he died, former U.S. Commissioner of Education Ernest Boyer told me that he wished he could have written a book that told students and parents what they *really* needed to know about college. He said that he was glad that I was going to write it. This encouragement, from one of America's most respected educators, was a major inspiration.

I equally appreciate my many guinea pigs on whom I tried the ideas in this book: the students of Berkeley and Skyline High Schools, and, of course, my private clients.

Some of the busiest, most talented college counselors on earth took the time to review the manuscript: Steve Antonoff, Marsha Irwin, Mary Jane Kravets, Phyllis Steinbrecher, and Kal Chany. Colleen Rush and Jennifer Trussell added spicy editorial tidbits, and some noneducators helped make sure it all made sense to just plain parents: David Wilens, Ray Mattoon, Barbara Griffith, and Kelly Manzer.

I am thankful for the good people at Barron's, especially Grace Freedson for her open mind and promptness, Max Reed, and Tom Vanderberg, fine editors and mensches.

Finally, to my wife, Dr. Barbara Nemko, thank you for tolerating a workaholic husband.

Marty Nemko
Oakland, California

INTRODUCTION
Should You Bother Reading This Book?

There's a ton of college information out there. This book includes only the best of the best. Whether you're an A student or just a student, you'll know

✓ the specific colleges *you* should apply to. You'll develop your custom-tailored list right here in this book, no computer necessary. And your list will be more on target than a computer-generated list.

✓ how to get in without losing your mind.

✓ how to find the cash to pay for college. Did you know that two families with the same income and assets can get totally different amounts of financial aid from the same college? I'll show you how to get the most money you're legally entitled to.

✓ the keys to a great college experience: How to find the best professors, get good grades, make friends, get along with your roommate, manage your time, and graduate with a good job or get into a good graduate school—having a good time all along the way.

I'll focus on the important information that isn't widely known. For example, do you know

✓ there are easier routes into prestigious colleges, for example, U.C. Berkeley's extension program, or Harvard's evening bachelor's programs.

✓ whether you'd do better on the SAT I or the ACT?

✓ whether you should sign up for an expensive SAT/ACT preparation course?

✓ if it's better to get an A in a regular class or a B in an honors class?

✓ that almost 40 percent of students surveyed at the nation's designer-label colleges believed their college wasn't worth the money. (There may be wiser choices than brand-name schools and I'll tell you about them!)

✓ how to ensure that your essay reveals your best self?

✓ that the college rankings published in major news magazines can be grossly misleading?

✓ that a letter from a college encouraging you to apply does not indicate that it will admit you?

✓ that there are ways to apply to lots of colleges with just one application?

✓ whether you should go straight to college or not? (See page 201.)

✓ how to find a cool career?

✓ how to pick a major you'll be happy with?

✓ easy ways to meet new friends at college?

As your friendly college coach, I will share all that and much more with you. I've even included tips for parents that can prevent lots of stress.

Rather than read this book cover to cover, treat it as an encyclopedia: Look up what you need when you need it. When you're ready to choose a college, read that section. When you're ready to think about the SAT, read that section. When you're sick of your college coach, slam me shut knowing you have me at your service whenever you need me, 24 hours a day, seven days a week.

Before we get to Job One (getting you a list of colleges at which you're most likely to be happy and successful), I'd better warn you what not to do. Literally millions of college-bound students have made the following mistakes.

Top Five Mistakes in Choosing a College

5. **Relying on the rankings in major news magazines.** It's absurd, but the rankings are based mainly on data that each college's administration itself submits. That's like *Rolling Stone* asking a singer to review her own CD. Not surprisingly, the *Wall Street Journal* has reported that some colleges fudge the data they submit.

   Even worse, these rankings are created totally without input from the most relevant persons of all: the colleges' students. Who do these magazines poll? College administrators, many of whom have never even visited most of the campuses they're asked to rate! Would you trust a restaurant rating written by a reviewer who had never seen the restaurant, let alone eaten there?

4. **Relying on a college's reputation.** Sure, if you're a straight A student with a 1500 SAT score, you might want to consider designer-label colleges like the Ivys or Stanford. But even many top students should think twice. Many prestigious colleges get their good reputations because their professors do a lot of research, because the colleges are large and therefore well known, and because of the good jobs many of their graduates get. None of these are great reasons to choose a college. Here's why.

> **"Big-name undergraduate colleges are not necessarily the best."**

Professors' research often lowers the quality of undergraduate education. For the $150,000 four-year cost, at research universities[1] (for example, Harvard, Yale, and Stanford), there are too many auditorium-sized classes taught by professors who care more about what's in their test tubes than what's in their students' heads.

Large: Bigger often means large classes, more red tape, and less individual attention.

Jobs and graduate schools. Yes, a designer label on a diploma is a plus in the job market. But Ivy-caliber students may get an equal or better advantage if they attend a less prestigious college, because there they are more likely to get top grades, personal attention, leadership opportunities, and superb letters of recommendation. My own daughter, who was admitted to Williams College, one of the nation's hardest-to-get-into colleges, instead opted for a less selective one. Because she was able to excel there, she got noticed by her professors, one of whom gave her a tip on a job in the White House. She ended up working for almost a year in Hillary Clinton's research office. Lest you think my daughter is an exception, 40 percent of the nation's CEO's got their undergraduate degrees at public universities. Bonus: Less selective colleges will often give a big scholarship to Ivy-caliber students.

In short, big-name undergraduate colleges are not necessarily the best. I'm not asking you to dismiss designer-label colleges, but it's worth keeping an open mind: learn about the many excellent but less well-known colleges I'll tell you about and then decide where to apply.

---

[1] A university basically means a large college that has graduate as well as undergraduate students.

3. **Relying on one person's opinion** (for example, your girlfriend, your uncle, or even your parent). The best decisions are usually made when you gather information from multiple sources. (I'll clue you in on easy ways to get the info you need. See Chapter 2.)

2. **Being too shy to ask questions.** You're buying an expensive product that will take four to six years of your life. You have the right to ask questions. Representatives from the colleges love to answer questions and so do college students. If someone was thinking of attending your high school and asked how you like it, wouldn't you tell the person? Don't know what to ask? Some questions that would make Sherlock Holmes proud are on pp. 26–28.

1. **Relying on a college's advertising:** campus tours, campus representatives visiting your high school, the stuff that fills your mailbox, interviews (yes, these too are advertising), get-togethers for admitted students, open houses, and handwritten notes or phone calls from a student or professor at the college. A few colleges even send top students an individualized video from the college president: "Hi, Mary. I'm really hoping you'll join us this fall." The amount of attention you get while a college is recruiting you (and it *is* recruiting you) does *not* indicate how much attention you'll get after you're enrolled at the college.

> **The amount of attention you get while a college is recruiting you (and it *is* recruiting you) does *not* indicate how much attention you'll get after you're enrolled at the college.**

Statistics trumpeted by the college are also advertising. For example, many brand-name universities report a faculty/student ratio of less than 20:1 even though the typical undergraduate spends much time in classes of 100+. How do colleges get away with it? They count classes you'll probably never take, for example, Advanced Sanskrit, and classes for Ph.D. students. They may even count professors who never teach anyone—they only do research. Remember, colleges are a business much like any other business. To sell, many colleges hide their negatives, stretch their positives, and as mentioned above, may even distort the truth.

Unfortunately, you must think of admissions representatives as salespersons, not as admissions counselors, which is what they like to call themselves. You may think I'm being harsh, but the fact is, admissions "counselors" rarely counsel a student not to apply. Too few are likely to say, for example, what a true counselor might: "I'm not sure this college is challenging enough for you. Why not apply to more selective colleges?" Admissions reps' job is to sell their college.[2]

Now here's the right way to choose a college.

---

[2] Questionable admissions practices are described in more detail in "Deny the Brutes," by Thomas Sturgeon, associate director of admission at Duke. *Journal of College Admission*, June 1995, pp. 16-23.

CHAPTER 1

Here Is Your Personalized List of Colleges

What I Want in a College

Directions: You'll end up with a better list of colleges if you and your parent(s) answer these questions together. Or do it solo and then see if your parents agree with your choices.

I'm willing to consider colleges that are

1. **(Circle one or both)**

   two-year

   four-year

   (Want help deciding? See p. 147.)

   Note: Many good students might consider starting at a two-year college.

2. filled with students who in high school were **(Choose one)**

   A students (1250–1600 SAT or 28–36 ACT)

   B to A students (1050–1250 SAT or 22–27 ACT)

   B students, but the colleges have honors programs to challenge A students

   B– to C+ students (900–1100 SAT or 18–21 ACT)

   (Want help deciding? See p. 150.)

   Note: Many good students might consider starting at a two-year college.

3. priced for four years, not counting financial aid, at \$_____or less.

   Here's a rough estimate of total costs including living expenses and not counting financial aid for four years of college:

   ✓ Prestige private colleges such as Princeton, Harvard, or Stanford: \$150,000

   ✓ Brand-name private colleges, for example, Carleton, Boston College, University of Miami: \$120,000

   ✓ Less well-known private colleges, for example, Creighton, Millsaps, Hillsdale: \$90,000

✓ Brand-name public colleges and those in high-cost states, for example, Berkeley, Michigan, SUNY-Binghamton: $60,000 in-state ($100,000 out-of-state)

✓ Less-well known public colleges in low-cost states, for example, Truman State, North Carolina-Asheville, most two-year public colleges: $45,000.
(Want help deciding? See p. 63 and p. 154.)

4. (Circle one or more)

small

large

have a living/learning program (sort of like a small college within a large one)

(Want help deciding? See p. 155.)

5. (Circle one or more)

in/near a big city

away from a big city

(Want help deciding? See p. 158.)

6. in specific state(s) or city(ies):_____

in specific regions:

(Circle one or more)

Northeast

South

Midwest

West

(Want help deciding? See p. 159.)

7. (Circle one or both)

offer many majors

that specialize

(Want help deciding? See p. 159.)

8. (Circle one or more)

conservative

moderate/diverse

liberal

(Want help deciding? See p. 160.)

9. (Circle one or more)

mixed gender and race

single gender

single race

(Want help deciding? See p. 161.)

10. (Circle one or both)

secular or not strongly religious

strongly religious

(Want help deciding? See p. 161.)

11. offer an academic calendar of
(Circle one or more)

quarters

semesters

4-1-4

block

(Want help deciding? See p. 162.)

12. If important to you, circle this: Co-op program

(Want help deciding? See p. 163.)

13. If important to you, circle this: Extensive disability services

(Want help deciding? See p. 163.)

Now, look over all the items you circled and put a star next to the few items you *most* want in your college.

IMPORTANT DIRECTIONS!
(They're simpler to follow than they look.)

It's impossible to look carefully at all of the nation's 3,500 colleges. So, first you have to decide on a manageable number (10–15) of colleges to consider that are potentially right for *you*. Here's how to do it quickly:

Step 1. Write down the names of any colleges you already know you want to consider. Maybe it's the college you've been dreaming about since preschool, the one your coach recommended or a parent attended, or a local college that fits what you circled on your *What I Want* list.

Step 2. Mark an X next to the **categories** below that fit the *What I Want* list you just created. Select enough categories so you have 20–30 colleges to choose from.

Two-Year Colleges

Northeast (10 of these are on p. 165)
South (1 of these is on p. 166)
Midwest (6 of these are on p. 166)
West (4 of these are on p. 166)

Four-Year Colleges Offering Many Majors
Mainly A Students
Small, Northeast, in/near big city (6 of these are on p. 167)
Small, Northeast, town (6 of these are on p. 167)
Small, South, in/near big city (1 of these is on p. 167)
Small, South, town (1 of these is on p. 167)
Small, Midwest, in/near big city (1 of these is on p. 167)
Small, Midwest, town (2 of these are on p. 167)
Small, West, in/near big city (3 of these are on p. 167)
Small, West, town (1 of these is on p. 168)

Large, Northeast, in/near big city (8 of these are on pp. 167–168)
Large, Northeast, town (2 of these are on p. 168)
Large, South, in/near big city (1 of these is on p. 168)
Large, South, town (1 of these is on p. 168)
Large, Midwest, in/near big city (1 of these is on p. 168)
Large, Midwest, town (1 of these is on p. 168)
Large, West, in/near big city (3 of these are on p. 168)

Mainly B to A Students

Small, Northeast, in/near big city (6 of these are on p. 168)
Small, Northeast, town (15 of these are on p. 169)
Small, South, in/near big city (5 of these are on p. 169)
Small, South, town (3 of these are on p. 170)
Small, Midwest, in/near big city (3 of these are on p. 170)
Small, Midwest, town (3 of these are on p. 170)
Small, West, in/near big city (1 of these is on p. 170)

Large, Northeast, in/near big city (7 of these are on p. 170)
Large, Northeast, town (6 of these are on p. 171)
Large, South, in/near big city (5 of these are on p. 171)
Large, South, town (1 of these is on p. 171)
Large, Midwest, in/near big city (3 of these are on p. 171)
Large, Midwest, town (2 of these are on p. 171)
Large, West, in/near big city (1 of these is on p. 172)
Large, West, town (2 of these are on p. 172)

Many B– Students

Small, Northeast, in/near big city (14 of these are on p. 172)
Small, Northeast, town (24 of these are on pp. 172–173)
Small, South, in/near big city (20 of these are on p. 174)
Small, South, town (18 of these are on pp. 174–175)
Small, Midwest, in/near big city (14 of these are on pp. 175–176)
Small, Midwest, town (27 of these are on pp. 176–177)
Small, West, in/near big city (15 of these are on p. 177)
Small, West, town (6 of these are on pp. 177–178)

Large, Northeast, in/near big city (13 of these are on p. 178)
Large, Northeast, town (10 of these are on pp. 178–179)
Large, South, in/near big city (12 of these are on p. 179)
Large, South, town (11 of these are on pp. 179–180)
Large, Midwest, in/near big city (19 of these are on p. 180)
Large, Midwest, town (6 of these are on p. 181)
Large, West, in/near big city (12 of these are on p. 181)
Large, West, town (8 of these are on pp. 181–182)

Four-Year Colleges That Specialize

Military (5 of these are on p. 182)
Engineering & Physical Sciences (15 of these are on pp. 182–183)
Business (3 of these are on p. 183)
Visual Arts (10 of these are on pp. 183–184)
Performing Arts (11 of these are on p. 184)

Step 3. Turn to the page listed for the categories you've just chosen. Use the information provided there about each college to narrow your list to 10–15 colleges. If you know you'll want an unusual major or sport, narrow to 15–20 colleges rather than 10–15.

Step 4. If you have a college counselor, get his or her reaction to your list. You might cross-check your list against the one generated for you at:

www.csearch.kaplan.com

Step 5. To find out which of your selected colleges actually fit you and are of high quality, turn to page 8.

CHAPTER 2
How to Judge a College

Presto, change-o, in Chapter 1 you narrowed your search from 3,500 to 10 to 15 colleges. Now here's how to further pare down your list to the 3 to 10 you'll actually apply to.

First, an Insider's Secret

Ninety-five percent of colleges need you more than you need them. Why? Because, believe it or not, most colleges never fill all their slots. If you enroll, that's money they wouldn't otherwise have. If in September, you called colleges and said, "I'd like to start *next*

week but can only afford *half* of your tuition," many *good* colleges would say, "Send in an application and we'll see what we can do."

Moral of the story: Be picky. Choosing a college is like buying clothes. There are hundreds

> **If you said, "I'd like to start *next week* but can only afford *half* of your tuition," many *good* colleges would say, "Send in an application and we'll see what we can do."**

of garments to choose from. You're trying to figure out which give you the best quality and fit for the money. This chapter tells you how to do it.

It *is* worth reading this entire chapter. But I know that some of you won't do that, so, although it hurt me to do it, I've written the 60-second McVersion of this chapter. It's on page 40.

Step 1: Keep a College Notebook

Take a section of your school notebook with 10 to 15 pages, and label it "colleges." Then write the names of the 10 to 15 colleges on your list, one on the top of each page, for example, Moo U., I.O.U., Catatonic State.

Step 2: Use an On-Line or Print College Directory

Find out which of the 10 to 15 colleges on your list offer your desired major(s), sport, honors program, and so on. How do you find out? Just visit *www.collegeEdge.com.* It has detailed info on 6,000 colleges. Similar information is provided at *www.college-quest.com* and *www.collegeboard.org.* Or go low tech: Look up each of your colleges in one of those big college directories such as *Barron's Profiles of American Colleges.* To do a head-to-head comparison of your candidate schools, visit *www.usnews.com/usnews/edu/college/coworks.htm* on the Web.

If a college doesn't offer your major, sport, or an honors program, note that in your college notebook, or even cross the college off your list. Warning to athletes: Unless you're a true pro prospect, be sure to choose a college first because it's a good fit academically and socially, and second because you'd enjoy playing sports there.

You might be saying, "But I don't know what I want to major in." Not to worry. I'll show you how to find the right major, a cool career, even decide if you want to play a college varsity sport—all in just a few pages. (Those few pages may be the most useful in this entire book, pp. 195–199.)

By the way, most colleges' Web sites are filled with all sorts of other information: everything that's in its catalog, homepages of campus student groups, campus event schedules, photographs of the campus, copies of the campus newspaper, and maybe a campus directory so you can e-mail questions to students, faculty, and coaches. Great source!

If you want the inside story on a college, check out its student newspaper on-line; or if it's not on-line, call the college and ask the student newspaper office to mail you a few copies. College newspapers from all around the nation are available at:

yahoo.com/News_ and_Media/Newspapers/College_and_University
http://beacon-www.asa.utk.edu/resources/papers.html

Step 3: Read About Your Colleges in a Guide That Reports Student Opinions

This may be the smartest way to judge a college's quality and fit.

✓ *The Best 311 Colleges* offers a two-page writeup that distills what more than 100 randomly selected students think of their college.

✓ *The Fiske Guide to Colleges* offers three- to four-page essays on 300 colleges based on a small number of student questionnaires and one submitted by an administrator. These essays offer different information: strong majors, special programs, details about out-of-class life, and a description of the physical campus and surroundings.

✓ *Barron's Guide to the Most Competitive Colleges* offers a 10–15 page essay on each of 50 hard-to-get-into colleges, written by one student or recent alum.

✓ *Barron's Best Buys in College Education* offers profiles that meld student opinion with useful statistics. Another plus is that it covers many colleges not profiled in other guides.

> **If you simply choose 3 to 10 favorite colleges to apply to based on Steps 1 to 3, you've done a better job of choosing than most students.**

In the latter three guides, you won't find much negative information about any college because the queried students were hand-picked by each college's administration.

If you simply choose 3 to 10 favorite colleges to apply to based on Steps 1 to 3, you've done a better job of choosing than most students. Congratulations! But if you have a little more patience, it's worth doing at least some of the steps in the rest of this chapter.

IMPORTANT

This may seem odd, but throughout your college search, focus on the negative. Colleges will take care of presenting the positive. You'll soon notice that all brochures show picture-perfect weather and classes with no more than ten fascinated students. Yeah, right.

You can uncover a college's negative aspects by asking good questions of students during your virtual and actual visits. See pages 13–16 and 18–31.

Even *The Best 311 Colleges*, which surveys students virtually at random, can occasionally present an overly positive picture of a college. For example, at a major state university, a few days before the surveyors from *The Best 311 Colleges* were coming on campus to poll the students, the college's administration launched a campaign to let students know how important it was that the college came out looking good.

Step 4: Look at the Catalog

A hands-on copy is nice, but it often costs as much as a medium pizza and can take weeks to arrive. Alternatives: 9,000 college catalogs can be found at *www.cgf.org*, and some of the major public libraries have all the nation's catalogs on microfiche or on CD-ROM.

Here's what to look for in the catalog:

✓ Have you taken the high school courses and exams that the college requires?

✓ Are there enough professors in your intended major? The more there are to choose from, the easier it will be to find good ones, and to have plenty of course choices.

✓ Do the college courses in your prospective major sound interesting?

✓ Are there special programs that intrigue you? For example, a combination biology and business major?

✓ Does the college require you to take too many college courses you'd hate to take, either for your major or as a general graduation requirement? Can you handle calculus? More foreign language?

✓ How much credit toward your college degree will you get for your Advanced Placement or International Baccalaureate courses?

Step 5: Rent the Video

Don't bother with the videos that the colleges send to you or the video clips on computer-based products such as *CollegeView.* Those are commercials made by the colleges. The colleges spend big bucks to hire slick advertising firms to make those videos as seductive as possible. Watch them and you may end up choosing the best commercial rather than the best college.

The videos worth watching are put out by a crazy college counselor named Cliff Kramon. He was nutty enough to visit over 330 colleges, from Oxford in England to Harvey Mudd in California. With camcorder in hand, he simply took each college's tour and recorded it along with the questions he and others asked of the tour guide. You and as many family members and friends as you like get to tour as many colleges as you want, no matter how far away, in the comfort of your living room for just $15 a piece, the price of two movie tickets. If you're on a budget, rent videos only of colleges that you're thinking of dropping from your list. Order at *www.collegiatechoice.com* or (201) 871-0098.

The Klass Report College Video Tours are more professionally done but they're available only for 40 prominent colleges. They're $19.95 per school. Order at *klassreport.com.* or 800-699-1330.

There are cheesy but better-than-nothing "virtual tours" (usually captioned slides and/or maps) on hundreds of colleges free online at *www.campustours.com.*

Step 6: Make a Virtual Visit

In a virtual visit, you get to talk with the college's students without having to leave home.

Is this helpful? You betcha. You get personalized answers to your questions from random students rather than from college reps whose job is to sell the college to you. If you were about to buy a car, wouldn't you want to talk with someone who owns the same car, not just the salesperson? Students are in the best position to describe what student life on campus is really like.

You may fear you're imposing. You're not. Imagine that a student who was thinking of attending your high school asked what you thought of your school. Wouldn't you be willing to talk?

Don't worry, you won't seem geeky. Just think of it as sampling the goods before you buy.

How to get to talk with students? Easy. No need to trek all the way to campus. No matter which college, there's a supply of students just a phone call or e-mail away. Maybe you know a friend or relative at the college. Or perhaps your high school keeps a list of former students and the colleges they attend. Or see if the college's Web site allows you to e-mail students there. That's a great option if you're shy. Or contact an alumnus. Alumni are a great source of info about a college. They've spent years there and have the benefit of hindsight. Focus on recent graduates. Colleges change (slowly). There's a list of alumni of most colleges at *www.alumni.net* or at *www.branchout.com*

None of the above sound good? No problem. You can conduct your virtual visit on the phone. Just muster a little courage, phone the college switchboard (phone numbers for 434 colleges are on pp. 165–184) and ask to have the call transferred to a residence hall front desk. Most dorms have a student there to answer the phone.

To start the conversation, try something like, "Hi, I'm a high school student who is thinking about attending your college. I've read about it, but I thought I'd learn more by talking with some students. Do you like it?" Take notes. Ask a few other questions (see list on pp. 26–28), then ask if another student is around. If not, have the call transferred to another dorm, to the student government office, or student newspaper office. Don't get too swayed by a single student who either loves or hates the college.

You might also contact the department you're planning to major in. Explain that you're shopping for a college. Then ask if there's anything about the undergraduate program you should know that isn't in the catalog. That information might help you decide if that college is a good choice for you. You can then cite that information in your admission essay: "Happy Days College is a particularly good fit for me because I'm planning to major in psychology and your department specializes in physiological psychology, which is my main interest." If you're really lucky, your call to the department can even result in your contact putting a good word in for you with the admissions office—after all, you were motivated enough to check out the department, something that 99 percent of applicants aren't.

A PATCH OF IVY?

If you're interested in an honors program, call the switchboard and ask to be transferred to the honors office. Ask five questions: how many honors classes are offered each term? What out-of-classroom opportunities are there for students in the honors programs? Is there an honors residence hall? Do honors students get special privileges such as first crack at course registration? What does it take to get admitted to the program?

If after your virtual visit, you're still interested in the college, have the call transferred to the admissions office. Ask a few questions. (Or ask them on the college's Web site.)

My favorite questions for admission counselors (salespeople):

✓ How is this college different from other small (or large) rural (or urban) colleges?

✓ Are there any special programs or opportunities that help a student to have a particularly rewarding experience compared with other colleges?

> **Remember: at 95 percent of colleges, they need you more than you need them.**

✓ What percentage of students with my SAT/ACT score and high school grades graduate from your college within four years? Five years?

✓ What are students' most legitimate gripes about the college?

Again, if you're feeling too shy to ask, remember that the college isn't too shy to ask for your $40,000 to $150,000 and four to six years of your life. You're entitled to quality information before buying. Don't be in awe of colleges. Remember, they are a business, and you're the customer they're trying to sell to. They don't want you to think that. They want you to think that slots at the college are hard to come by and you'd be lucky to get one. The fact is, it's the opposite. *Remember: at 95 percent of colleges, they need you more than you need them.*

Step 7: Apply to the Colleges

At this point, you probably have enough information to determine which 3 to 10 colleges to apply to. If you'd like even more information, do Step 8 and/or 9.

When you know you want to apply to a college, contact its admissions office. Web addresses and phone numbers for 434 nationally noteworthy colleges are on pp. 165–184. Nothing formal or fancy is required: simply say, "I'm a high school junior who is interested in your college. Please send me

✓ a viewbook"(the brochure for prospective students. You know, the one showing the perfect weather and the ten fascinated students).

✓ an application for admission." (It doesn't hurt to ask for two, just in case.) As you'll see on page 47, you may actually apply using a special application that allows you to apply to as many colleges as you like with just one basic application.

✓ an application for financial aid."

✓ housing information."

✓ a catalog." Or if they want to charge major bucks for it, you might just ask for a brochure on the major and any special program you're interested in, such as honors program, living-learning program, or learning disability services.

✓ a few copies of the student newspaper."

✓ a copy of the college's most recent student satisfaction survey" (INSIDER'S SECRET and my favorite). If they send it to you, you get to find out how hundreds of students feel about dozens of aspects of the college. If they won't send it to you, maybe they don't want you to see how dissatisfied the students are. If they say they don't conduct student satisfaction surveys, perhaps they don't care enough about how satisfied their students are.

HOW MANY COLLEGES SHOULD YOU APPLY TO?

Most students apply to too few colleges. One reason to apply to more is that it can help you negotiate: "I'd like to come to your college, but it's just too expensive. FatCat College offered me $5,000 more financial aid." Yes, often you can negotiate financial aid.

And remember, it may not be much more work to crank out a few more applications. An essay for one college can often be used for another. Also, as I mentioned, there are special applications that enable you to apply to many colleges with one basic form. (See p. 47.)

✓ **If you prefer and are potentially admissible to colleges with mainly A students, apply to**

  five to seven colleges with mainly A students. (These schools are tough to get into, so you need to apply to at least five to increase your chances of getting into at least one.)

  two to three colleges that you can count on getting into. Choose these safe colleges as carefully as the others. You may end up there! One safe college should also be financially safe—a college at which you're confident you'll be admitted and sure your family can comfortably afford.

THE PERFECT PARENT: As early as possible, candidly discuss with your college-bound scholar how much cash you're willing to cough up over the 4 to 6 years of college and how much debt you're willing to take on.

✓ **If you prefer and are potentially admissible to colleges with some B and some A students, apply to**

  three to five colleges with some B and some A students

  two to three colleges with many B– students that you can count on getting into. Choose these safe colleges as carefully as the others. You may end up there! One safe college should also be financially safe— a college at which you are confident you'll be admitted and sure your family can afford.

✓ **If you prefer and are potentially admissible to colleges with many B– to C+ students or two-year colleges, apply to**
three to five of those. Be sure to include one financially safe college—one at which you're confident you'll be admitted and sure your family can afford.

Step 8: College Fairs

Sure, college fairs are convenient because many colleges send representatives there. But remember that you'll be talking with the colleges' salespeople. Even so, they can be somewhat useful if you know what to ask.

Don't ask questions designed to dig up dirt because college reps usually won't cooperate. Questions likely to yield useful information include "What makes your college different than other small (large) rural (urban) colleges?," "What programs is the college particularly proud of?," "What sort of student is such a good fit for your college that you'd tell him it's worth coming across the country to attend?"

Take notes in your college notebook after visiting each college's representative. Otherwise, the colleges may blend together. Take very few brochures; they'll probably go unread into the recycling bin.

Step 9: Make an Actual Visit

You wouldn't marry someone you've never met. Yet many students commit to a college without checking it out in person. Mistake.

Don't worry about appearing out of place. Every year, thousands of high school students can be seen poking around college campuses with their dorky parents asking questions that make their children's faces red.

The main purpose of a visit is to see how you feel among these students. A pretty campus and fancy facilities are nice, but in the end, your happiness will depend more on how well you fit in. And a smart visit can help you judge that. Secondary purpose: if it's a college to which you're unsure you'll be admitted, a visit and on-campus interview can boost

> **Interview only if most adults enjoy talking with you.**

your chances. A visit shows that you're serious about attending, your answer to the essay question "Why this college?" will be more convincing, and if you interview well (see pp. 57–59 for interview tips), it may help a bit more. Usually interviews are *not* required. If it's optional, here's a rule of thumb: Interview only if most adults enjoy talking with you.

INSIDER'S SECRET: Many students make a worse decision after a visit than they would have without one. A college can feel so overwhelming that many students come away with little more than, "The campus was beautiful and the tour guide was nice." Too often, luck plays a big role. Did you show up on a rainy day? Get a terrific tour guide?

Here's how to make sure that your visit helps you make a wise choice.

WHEN TO VISIT

Consider fall of the senior year; you'll be applying soon so you'll be motivated to take your visit seriously, yet there's still time to add or subtract colleges from your list. Fall is the most popular time to visit, so to be sure you can get an interview and dorm stay, make an appointment one to three months in advance, especially if it's a college with mainly A students. An ideal time to visit? Late August or early September, when a college may be in session but your high school is not. But remind yourself of whether that balmy late summer weather will soon yield to a long, bone-chilling winter.

A good alternative, especially if you think you might interview poorly, and/or if you're applying to faraway colleges, is to wait until April of your senior year and visit your favorite two or three colleges that admitted you. An April visit means you don't waste trips on colleges that didn't admit you, and your motivation to check them out will be high. And you won't have the fear (a groundless one) that if you ask tough-minded questions, the college will reject you.

If you're a varsity athlete, consider visiting when your sport is in season.

Worst time to visit? Any time that classes aren't in session: on weekends, and especially during vacations. Visiting then is like test-driving a car with the engine off. Many colleges basically shut down for the weekend. Summer school students are different from the regular ones, and the tone of the place changes, so you'll get an inaccurate, yet hard-to-shake, impression.

Similarly, don't visit during Spring Carnival or Homecoming. That's not what the campus is usually like.

I have mixed feelings about campus open houses for prospective students. On the upside, there are lots of people around to make you feel welcome and answer your questions. But at open house, there usually is, as Bates College Vice President Bill Hiss says, "a festive atmosphere that is very different from daily campus life."

BEFORE THE VISIT

1. Go with at least one parent. There's a lot to see and four or six eyes can see more than two. Also, it's fun to compare notes. However, when parents get a load of the naked parties and keggers, they somehow lose their open-mindedness about that college.

THE PERFECT PARENT: Family visits to colleges can be tough days of concentrated togetherness, especially when such a big decision is at stake: your money, their future. Your kid may "hate" you at this age. Meanwhile, you're reminiscing about your good ol' college days, freaking out about your kid leaving, and stressing about having to jeopardize your financial security for the privilege of having a college corrupt your baby. It's a situation ripe for disaster. These ground rules can help:

✓ Agree on how much time you and your child will be separate during your college visit. Many families agree to take the tour together, then separate for a few hours, meet again briefly, then separate again.

✓ Agree that when you're together, it's okay for parents to ask an occasional question but not a nonstop barrage.

✓ Ask your child if there are things she specifically wants you to do or not do. For example, teens often go wild with embarrassment when Mom gives a good-bye kiss.

Just go with friends? Usually fun; only sometimes useful. Some students find it too tempting to goof around.

2. Plan to visit only one and certainly no more than two colleges per day. If it's a school you're serious about, spend an entire evening in a dorm.

3. If you're visiting more than one college, try to save your top choice(s) for last. As you go along, you'll learn how to visit and interview more effectively.

4. Call ahead.

✓ Ask whether your selected dates coincide with Homecoming, Parents Weekend, the first week of class, finals week or other inappropriate times for a visit.

✓ Ask the admissions office if you can spend the night in a dorm, perhaps with a student in your prospective major. (Bring a sleeping bag.) This serves a second purpose: It lets the admissions office know that you're seriously considering this college. It likes admitting students who are likely to show up in September.

✓ Make motel reservations for Mom and Dad (unless you'd like them to sleep in the dorm with you).

✓ If you want an interview, make an appointment. If you have a prospective major, schedule an interview with a professor in that department. Not only will you learn about the department, but if you're impressive (or if the department is hungry for students), the professor may put in a good word for you with admissions office.

✓ Get travel and parking directions. It feels terrible to arrive clueless and nervous at a strange campus. I've seen families unfairly turned off to a college just because they got off to a bad start. You can get point-to-point directions free on-line at *www.mapquest.com.*

✓ If the college's sticker price will strain your family's budget, make an appointment with the financial aid officer. Be sure to read Chapter 4 first.

✓ If you're an athlete, musician, or actor, ask the admissions office to give you an appointment with the coach or director.

5. On the way to the college, reread your notes on that school, college guide write-ups on the college, and material the college sent you.

DURING THE VISIT

Beware of tour guides, the time, the weather, and the physical campus. Here's why.

Tour Guides

Tour guides are almost always enthusiastic, unless, of course, they're in a bad mood, neither of which, of course, affects whether you would be happy at this college.

Time

If you happen to visit a college at noon, that's when most colleges are most alive. Students are buzzing around campus amid folks hawking hand-crafted jewelry or urging you to join their clubs or causes, all perhaps accompanied by a rock band. But arrive at 4:30, and even the most dynamic college won't seem as exciting.

Weather

No matter how great the college, rain, not to mention slush, can't help but dampen enthusiasm for it. Think about the *typical* weather at the college, not that day's weather.

The Physical Campus

It's easy to be awed by ivy-covered walls, lush lawns, and chiming bell towers. But for most people, the campus' attractiveness ends up having a modest impact on their happiness and success. As a student at the lovely University of the South said, "The beauty wears off, so if you don't have a better reason for going to that college, you may be in trouble." Remember, manicured lawns and pristine buildings are ultimately paid for by students. When you realize that your tuition cash is being blown on shrubs, you may not find it so beautiful.

So, as soon as you arrive, say aloud three times:

✓ I won't let the tour guide sway me.

✓ I won't let the day's weather sway me.

✓ I won't let the college's brand name sway me.

✓ I won't let the campus's beauty (or lack thereof) sway me too much. (Don't be like one of my clients, whose family drove six hours to visit a college, took one look, and insisted that his father turn around without ever having left the car. He found the buildings "sterile-looking.")

I will do at least some of the following:

Bring a memo pad.

See something you want to remember about the college? Write it down right then. Otherwise, it's easy to forget, and in a week, colleges start to melt together. Was it Mary Washington College or Ramapo College that had those great instructors? Also, you'll be able to jot down the names, phone numbers, and e-mail addresses of students and professors you met so you can ask follow-up questions.

Take pictures.

Take pictures of what you want to remember about the college: the inspirational professor, the student that typifies the place, the dorm that looks like a bomb hit it, the great recreational sports facilities, the chicken tetrachloride. Begin with a picture of something with the college's name on it (for example, the college's main gate), or you'll forget which college goes with which pictures. Think you'll feel like a raging dork with a camera? Remember, the only difference between you and them is that they're enrolled dorks. Besides, if you do enroll, they'll never remember you. All dorks look alike.

Take the tour.

Try to do it early in your visit. It will orient you. But remember that the tour guide is probably giving a spiel scripted by the admissions office. Answers to questions that might put the college in a bad light—"How's the crime rate?"—are also often scripted. Before you get impressed with the fancy equipment that he shows you, ask yourself or the tour guide how often you are likely to be using it.

> **"On your tours, what do you try to emphasize and deemphasize about the college?"**

Before you get impressed with the world-class researchers, ask whether they're really good teachers or just good researchers, and how much are you likely to be taught by them.

My favorite question for the tour guide: "On your tours, what do you try to emphasize and deemphasize about the college?" (See pp. 26–28 for other questions.)

After the tour.

If your parent is with you, split up for at least part of the time. Divide the detective work, then meet every so often to compare notes and figure out what to do next.

INSIDER'S SECRET: *Never leave a college campus without asking questions of at least seven students that the admissions staff did NOT put in front of you.* Don't just speak with who's paid by the college, speak with who's paying the college. In addition to getting the straight scoop, you'll feel what it's like to be around this college's students. Here are some ways to find them.

Grab 'em. I know it's scary, but approach friendly looking students at a campus hangout (student union, plaza, dorm recreation room, cafeteria, coffee house) and ask a question or two. Most students love to talk about their school. You might start with something like, "I'm thinking of coming to this college and thought I should talk with some students. What should I know about it that I couldn't find out in the official brochure?"

Eavesdrop. Listen in on a few cafeteria tables' conversation. Do you like these students? Could you imagine yourself in a discussion like that? (Are people talking about issues other than whether *ER* is a good show?) When you feel brave, go over to a group of students, tell them that you're a high school student considering this college, and are trying to learn more about what it's like. They'll probably clue you in on all sorts of stuff and be more open than you'd expect. After all, they were in your shoes not long ago.

More cafeteria clues. While you're in the cafeteria, sample the food. Tasty morsels or mystery meat? If you're vegetarian, is there more than a salad bar and soggy veggies?

Most colleges claim to celebrate diversity. The cafeteria is a great place to assess the reality because, there, integration is voluntary. Do people of different races eat together or do they self-segregate?

Drop by the student newspaper office. Newspaper folk are excellent sources of information about a college. Also, pick up a few copies of the campus newspaper. What stories make the front page? What's in the letters to the editor? What's on the campus calendar of events?

How to visit ten classes in a half hour.

Sitting in on one class can be misleading—the professor could be a campus star or a campus joke. Instead, ask someone to point out a building in which a wide range of undergraduate classes is taught, especially those in your prospective major.

INSIDER'S SECRET: Stroll down the halls and peek in five to ten back doors, or duck in the back row of a large lecture class. (People do it all the time. Some even get grades.) Are most professors interesting or are they the answer to your insomnia problem? Do the students seem involved or are you seeing heads about to crash on desktops? Spend a minute in back of five or ten classes and you'll get the picture.

Some students say they're too shy to stand outside a classroom door or duck into the back row of a large class, but it's worth conquering the shyness. Shouldn't you sample a few classes before buying four to six years worth? Don't be surprised. Many students do take five and even six years to graduate.

Check out the quality of the program in your prospective major.

Ask the secretary in the office of your prospective major to point you to an *advanced* class in that major that will be ending in a few minutes. Head over there and wait for the class to be dismissed. Then stop a group of students and ask a question like, "I'm thinking of coming to this college and majoring in X. What's the major like? Do most graduates get good jobs or into good graduate schools?"

Look at the bulletin boards.

They are windows to the soul of a campus. Which flyers are most common: political action rally, expensive stereos for sale, semi-formal dances?

Check out the facilities.

For example, the on-campus housing, the recreational basketball courts, student center, dining halls, libraries, and so on.

What's near the campus?

Stroll through the blocks next to campus. Lots of bookstores, coffee houses, movie theaters? Affordable stores? Do you feel safe walking the streets? How easy is it to get to the nearest big city?

Spend a night in the dorm.

I know it's an uncomfortable thought. "I'm a high school kid. I'll feel weird spending a whole night with college students." Luckily, it usually ends up being fun as well as informative. A bunch of students will probably cluster around you, dying to reveal the inside joys and the inside dirt. Rats in the dorm? They've been seen even in ritzy colleges' dorms, but you won't learn that in the official brochure. You'll also see what the students are like. Too studious? Too raunchy? Too radical? Too preppy? Is the atmosphere like Animal House, an academic sweatshop, or a good balance? Life can vary a lot from dorm to dorm, so around 10 or 11 P.M. visit a couple of others.

MASTER LIST OF QUESTIONS TO ASK ABOUT A COLLEGE

It may be safest to ask students, not admissions officers, the most probing of these questions, but don't be intimidated.

Many students fear that if they ask a hard question of an admissions representative, they won't be admitted. Sure, if you ask five, you might be perceived as a problem, but ask a tough question or two and, if anything, your chances of being admitted will increase. The college will respect you for being a good consumer.

General Questions

What are some good and bad things about the college?

Do you feel the college is worth the money?

What sorts of students fit best and worst here?

What should I know about the college that wouldn't appear in the official brochure?

What legitimate gripes do students have about the college?

Why do students transfer out?

If you could do it again, would you choose this college?

Describe yourself. Then ask what the college is like for people like you. For example, "I'm shy, enjoy discussing intellectual things, and African American. How well would I fit here? What would I have to do to fit well?" Other ways you might characterize yourself: artsy, intellectual, social, religious, liberal, not materialistic, love sports, study five hours a night, a free spirit.

Academics

How good are the professors?

What's the typical class size?

Is it easy to get into the classes you want?

What are some outstanding majors?

Do you get to hear diverse perspectives or mainly just the liberal or just the conservative point of view?

How easy is it to get a professor to take a real interest in you?

Are there many opportunities for students to work one-on-one with faculty: for example, independent studies or working on faculty research?

Are the dorm rooms wired into the campus computer network?

I have a learning disability. What accommodations are made? (Ask this at the disabled student services office.)

Campus Life

What are the best housing options?

How good is the orientation for new students?

What's it like in the dorms?

Does overcrowding ever force the college to cram three students into a dorm room built for two, or even to force students to live in local motels?

Is it quiet enough to study in most dorm rooms?

How many hours a week do most students study?

How's the food?

What's the weather like?

What's it like for minorities (or gays, adult students, etc.)?

Are there many commuting students? Does that make the campus too quiet?

What do most students do on the weekends?

Is there much political activism?

How big a role do alcohol or drugs play in social life?

How big a role do fraternities and sororities play in campus life? If you're not in one, what are your social options?

Do you need a car?

What are big issues on campus?

Is safety an issue? (Also, ask the local police department for the crime statistics on and near campus. Most campus crime occurs near, not on campus.)

Athletes and musicians ask coaches: How much will I get to play?

Athletes and musicians ask other players: What's the coach (or director) like?

What does the college do to help ensure that graduating students find good jobs?

RIGHT AFTER YOU LEAVE CAMPUS

Complete the College Visit Report Card on p. 31. You may think you'll remember how you feel about the college, but it's safer to write it down immediately.

Consider writing a thank-you note to the admissions staff member who met with you. It can be as simple as:

Dear X,
Thanks for taking the time to meet with me. I enjoyed our discussion about _____. Thanks for helping me learn more about Utopia College. I'm glad you were impressed that I *[insert something she liked about you]*.

Looking forward to a fat envelope,

Sincerely,

Make a Copy of the Following for Each College You'll Visit

My Visit to _____ College

(Take this with you on your visit. When it's complete, attach it to the page in your notebook for this college.)

Previsit Information

Directions to campus and the interview:

Name(s) of person I am to interview with:

Date and time(s) of interview:

Time of tour:

Name and phone number of student I'll be staying with:

Where and when to find this student:

Questions I want to ask of students:

Questions I want to ask of college representatives:

COLLEGE VISIT REPORT CARD

Academic Life: Excellent   Good   Fair   Poor

Comments:

Campus Life: Excellent   Good   Fair   Poor

Comments:

The Students: Ideal   Good   Fair   Poor

Comments:

Overall Impression: Excellent   Good   Fair   Poor

Comments:

Step 10: Decide Among the Colleges That Admitted You

The best decision is usually one in which you gather lots of information and then go with your gut feeling. In most cases, just reread your notes on the colleges in your college notebook, run your decision by your college counselor, and compare costs. Be sure to take your financial aid award into account, especially the cash part (pp. 75–76 tells you how to do this).

INSIDER'S SECRET: If you're not satisfied with your financial aid award, negotiate or have your parent negotiate with the college's **director** of financial aid. Often, you can get more aid, especially if you provide new information. For example, another college offered you a better deal, your family has big medical or home repair expenses, or a divorce is impending. For more on negotiation, see p. 76.

If, by the May 1 deadline, you haven't received financial aid awards from all the colleges you applied to, ask for an extension from the colleges you're still considering. Usually, it will be granted. Don't say yes to a college until you've gotten financial aid offers from all colleges that offered to admit you. They can vary wildly!

> **Don't say yes to a college until you've gotten financial aid offers from all colleges that offered to admit you. They can vary wildly!**

Think twice about getting advice at the last minute. At this stage, you're vulnerable. A single person's comment can outweigh a year of investigation.

If you haven't been admitted anywhere, see p. 36.

When it's actually time to make your final decision, it's tempting to simply choose a brand-name college, even if you're not really sure it's the wisest choice, let alone worth the money. Earlier I've explained why brand-name colleges may indeed be overrated and overpriced, but perhaps another dose of caution might help here at the moment of truth. A study reported in the *American Economic Review* said, "While sending your child to Harvard may appear to be a good investment, sending him to a local state university to major in engineering and take lots of math and preferably attain a high G.P.A. is an even better investment. Apparently, what matters most is not which college you attend, but what you did while you were there…Measured college effects are small, explaining just one to two percent of the variance in earnings."

Loren Pope, author of *Colleges That Change Lives*, writes, "In March, 1994, *The New York Times* reported that a quarter of Harvard's class of 1958 had lost their jobs, were looking for work, or on welfare, just when their careers should have been cresting." The story went on, "Many in the class of '58 thought their degrees ensured career success. They were wrong." The autobiographical sketches written for the 35th reunion "did not radiate with expressions of success and optimism," said author and Yale professor Erich Segal. "Quite the contrary, they seemed like a litany of loss and disillusion." And Harvard was not alone. Alumni groups at other Ivy League schools, the story added, "are reporting that their members in growing numbers are suffering from the upheavals in corporate America. If there is a lesson in all this it is that a degree from a college like Harvard is no longer the lifetime guarantee of success in careers that it used to be."

Charles Eliot, former president of Harvard University, said, probably only half joking, "It is true that Harvard has become a storehouse of knowledge. The freshmen bring so much and the seniors take away so little."

I frequently pick on Harvard because it's considered the ultimate designer-label college. But the same criticisms could equally be leveled at all the big-name colleges: the other Ivys, Stanford, Northwestern, even the smaller prestige colleges, such as Amherst, Williams, and Oberlin.

Puhleeze, pick your college, not based on brand name, but on the good information this chapter has taught you how to obtain.

THE PERFECT PARENT: Too often, at this point, all the care in selecting the right colleges can go up in smoke. Johnny decides he wants to go to the college his friends are going to. Janie gets scared she might get lonesome so, at the last minute, she decides to stay close to home. Jose hears some student rave about College X and suddenly he ignores all his research and decides that College X is the perfect choice. Your job at this point is to be a calming influence. Remind your child of how he had identified his top-choice colleges.

If You're Wait-Listed at Your First-Choice College

You'll probably be as successful at your last-choice college as at your first. Your success will depend much more on what you do than on where you do it. But if you're convinced that you'd be much happier at a college that wait-listed you, do some or more of the following.

1. **Send a deposit** to a college at which you were admitted. That way you know you have somewhere to go in September.

2. **Call or have your counselor call the college** to find out why Choice #1 failed to recognize your awesome potential. If you need financial aid, be sure to find out if there's ample financial aid for wait-listed students who later get admitted. (Don't count on it.) Be sure all your financial aid information has been filed with that college.

3. **E-mail, fax, or overnight mail a letter** that expresses your disappointment at being wait-listed. (You needn't tell them that you've been sobbing for days.) Give specific reasons why this college is such a good fit, that you will definitely come if admitted and—if you need financial aid—it gives you a reasonable amount.

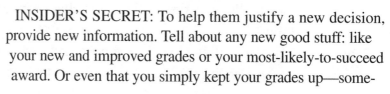

INSIDER'S SECRET: To help them justify a new decision, provide new information. Tell about any new good stuff: like your new and improved grades or your most-likely-to-succeed award. Or even that you simply kept your grades up—something not all second-semester seniors can claim. Also try to counter the college's objection to you. If the college turned you down because of a weak essay, offer to submit another. If it was a low math SAT, send a letter of recommendation from a math teacher. If they thought your extracurricular activities were lame, check to see if you've described them as well as you can. If they didn't like your grades, let them know if you improved in your senior year—one more reason that the second half of the senior year counts.

4. Call the admissions office, reminding them that additional material has been added to your file. Ask that your file be reviewed when the next batch of wait-listed students is being considered.

5. Consider a personal appearance (pronounced "plea").

If you're absolutely dying to go to this college, try one or more of the following.

INSIDER'S SECRETS: If possible, say that you are flexible with regard to major, and if an opening is available in a related area, you would accept that.

If campus housing is tight, offer to live off-campus. Or if the college is having trouble filling the dorms, agree to live on campus.

Ask if you can enroll on a nonmatriculated basis (an unofficial student) and if you get good grades the first term, become officially enrolled next term.

Ask if you could be admitted for the spring or summer term. Often there's more room then.

Ask if you could enroll at a branch campus for the first term, and if your grades are good, transfer to the main campus in the spring.

If you're unbelievably eager and your family can afford it, forgo financial aid. Think three times before offering to do this. Rarely is a college that much better a choice to justify forgoing aid. And yes, that includes Harvard, Yale, Stanford, and so on.

Pat Ordovensky, author of *Getting into College*, advises that if within two weeks you don't get a strong indication that you will eventually be accepted, you're better off forgetting your first-choice college. The fact is, most applicants on wait lists never get off.

AN EDITORIAL

One of colleges' many unfair-to-students practices is their use of the wait list. Many colleges put hundreds of students on the wait list, most of whom never get admitted. Why do colleges put so many students on the wait list, keeping their hopes up in vain? For reasons that make life more convenient for the college, the student be damned.

Some colleges do a lousy job of predicting how many students will show up in September, so they cover their incompetence by putting lots of students on the wait list. If they admit hundreds too few students, no problem. Just go to the wait list. If they guessed right, so what if hundreds of students' hopes are dashed?

Colleges know that students on the wait list are often desperate to get in—we all want what we can't have. So many wait-listed students agree to forego financial aid to get admitted. That's music to many colleges' ears: better to have a wait-listed student willing to pay full fare than an admitted student who wants a discount. Cynical souls wonder if some colleges deliberately admit fewer students than they need and put the rest on the wait list knowing that many will come begging: "Oh, please accept me off the wait list. I'll give up financial aid, I'll take a less desirable major, I'll give up my first-choice residence hall. Oh, just please take me!"

Rather than rejecting a weak student who is the child of a big donor, a bigwig, or a minority, some colleges give a courtesy wait-listing to allow the family to save face.

IF ALL THE COLLEGES HAVE SOMEHOW OVERLOOKED YOUR WONDERFULNESS

Even if they all turned you down, you still have options.
INSIDER'S SECRET: Each May, the National Association for College Admission Counseling (*www.nasac.com/news.html/*) issues a list of hundreds of four-year colleges that still need students for September. Many colleges will take a student as late as the second week of class! So will most two-year colleges, which may be one of the best choices of all.

Senioritis

If, in your senior year, you're fighting with your parents more than Moammar the Mauler fights with Ivan the Hulk, or find that you're doing less homework than you did in the first grade, you may have senioritis. Sure, it can be caused by thinking the second half of the senior year doesn't count.[1] But it may be that you're unconsciously distancing yourself from your high school and family life so you can feel better about going off to college.

There's no easy cure for senioritis. A corny but decent solution is to keep sharing thoughts and feelings with your parents, and try to compromise. There's only one thing I hope you don't make your parents compromise about. If you're doing something that can hurt yourself (like alcohol or drug abuse), consider letting your parents do what's needed to stop it.

Time-Out

Sick of school? Many college students look back and feel that they wasted their freshman year. *Effective* and *fun*: To help ensure that your freshman year isn't a waste, consider an **interim** semester or year.

If you ask your first-choice college to defer your admission for a semester or year, they'll probably say yes as long as you have something worthwhile planned. Each year, 50 or more students admitted to Harvard defer their admission.

Or if you were turned down by your top-choice schools, an interim year can often change their mind about you.

THE PERFECT PARENT: I know you're worried that if your child takes time out, she won't go back to college. However, as long as the interim semester/year is well planned the odds are excellent that not only will your child return to college, but she will

---

[1] Wrong. An offer of admission can be withdrawn if grades drop significantly. And most Canadian universities make their decisions *after* the 12th grade. Besides, the main reason you're in school is not to get grades, it's so you can have a better life. You may not believe me, but I swear it's true.

get more out of it. If you think your child is at risk of blowing off her first year of college, encourage an interim semester or year.

First, there are do-it-yourself interim programs. One of my clients simply got a Eurorail Pass, a copy of *Let's Go*, and explored Europe for a few months. Another shadowed a physician for one week, a journalist for the second week, an architect for the third, and an urban planner for the fourth. She liked the physician's week best, but decided that rather than helping people with cures that already exist, she'd rather develop new cures. So, she talked her way into a gofer job at a local biotech company. That strengthened her interest in medical research, so she applied to colleges with good molecular biology programs, and was accepted at a more prestigious college than she could have hoped for before her interim year.

A student who enjoys helping people might spend an interim year teaching an illiterate adult to read, as a Big Brother or Sister to a needy child, as a caretaker for a home-bound old person, or all of the above. Most major cities have a volunteer bureau that can help you find opportunities that interest you. If you can get a slot, consider joining AmeriCorps, sort of a domestic Peace Corps. You'll work on service projects with other young adults and receive a stipend for your efforts.

Then there are the structured interim programs. *Taking Time Off, Time Out*, and *Summer Options for Teenagers* describe hundreds of semester-long and year-long opportunities in addition to summer programs. Interim specialist Neil Bull suggests a few favorites from among the 2,000 in his database.

> *Environmentalists can work in the Student Conservation Association, which places students in outdoor volunteer programs across the United States. Students interested in health care can try the Frontier Nursing Service, which provides a chance to help people in rural Kentucky. Those looking for overseas experiences can explore the International Internship Network. Whether you are interested in art, finance, or wine making, you can be placed in Spain, Israel, Germany, France, or Italy. Students seeking a more traditional academic year in a foreign culture can choose from among many boarding schools throughout England, India, and Australia.*

For the typical students, two to four of these placements constitute the interim year. An example: Lex Leeming was admitted to Tufts University but felt burned out from school and knew if he went to college, he wouldn't do well. It was a perfect time to get away without losing any ground. So, Leeming spent a year far from conventional classrooms: building a log cabin on a ranch in Wyoming, helping a documentary filmmaker in upstate New York, serving an apprenticeship in a dive shop in Micronesia, and working as a gardener on the Italian island of Elba. "When I came back, I was totally psyched for my studies," said Leeming, now a sophomore at Tufts. "The year recharged my batteries, my motivation for college, my desire for work. I was excited about life."

Two specialists in planning a good-fit interim year are Neil Bull on the East Coast (617-547-0980, *www.interimprograms.com*) and David Denman on the West Coast (415-332-1831).

Worried that if you take a year off, you won't go back? David Denman says that among the hundreds of students he's worked with, only two haven't gone back to college.

The New York Times reported on a survey of hundreds of students at Phillips Academy (the prestigious private high school in Andover, Massachusetts) who had taken an interim year between high school and college. All the respondents said that if they had to do it over again, they would.

Beware: An interim year in which you simply sleep late, watch soap operas, slice sausage at the pizza shop, and party doesn't count. The odds of you having a rewarding year—let alone ending up back in college—are small.

For more on helping you decide whether to take time out, see pages 201–203.

The Final Test

Here's a final test of how you feel about the college you've selected. Ask yourself:

Would I be happy living and learning with these types of students for four years?

Would I be happy with these professors for four years?

Would I be happy living in this environment for four years?

Will this college really help me achieve my goals?

Is this college worth the money?

If the answer to all five questions is yes, you've found a good new home. Congratulations.

The McVersion of Chapter 2: How to Judge a College

Here's the one-minute version of this chapter. It's better to read the whole chapter, but even if you just use this half page to decide which colleges to apply to, you'll choose more wisely than most students do.

The simplest yet most meaningful way to decide which of your 10 to 15 colleges to apply to is to read about them in one or more of these guides:

✓ *The Best 311 Colleges*

✓ *The Fiske Guide to Colleges*

✓ *Barron's Guide to the Most Competitive Colleges*

✓ *Barron's Best Buys in College Education*

After reviewing the guides, apply to those colleges that sound best. Believe it or not, that's a better approach than most students take.

But if you really want to choose a college the right way, go back and read the full version of this chapter. It even contains a few half-decent jokes.

CHAPTER 3

How to Get Into Killer Colleges Without Killing Yourself

What a pain! Complicated forms with boring questions. Parents on your case to just sit down and do it. You want to go to college but there's got to be a better way than filling out stupid forms. Maybe there is, but at the risk of sounding like our own parents, we've found this works.

—from the cover of the M.I.T. application form

"Highly qualified students are denied by the hundreds at competitive colleges. Admission officers at Stanford turned away 500 of the 800 valedictorians who applied last year. The Ivys and Nearly Ivys and Georgetown did too. Princeton is the first to admit that it turns away many students who are better than the ones it takes."

—Journal of College Admissions

"I am frustrated by the way the selective college admissions process diminishes so many of our children...Children needn't be whipsawed by what is arguably the most successfully marketed product in America."

—Bill Mayher, author of The College Admissions Mystique

Imagine that you wanted to buy a Toyota, but the salesperson said, "I'm sorry but before we can take your money, you must complete a detailed application so we can determine if you're among the 15 percent who are qualified to own one." You apply, wait months, and finally receive a fat envelope that says, "Congratulations, you have been selected!" Wouldn't you be even more eager to buy the car? Might you even be willing to pay more for the privilege of being in such an exclusive club?[1]

The same is true of a college. If it's hard to get into, it seems more desirable. That's ironic because, as explained earlier, less prestigious colleges may be as good or better, even for your career. Plus, less prestigious colleges don't require you to orchestrate your entire high school life just so it looks good on your college application, nor do they require stratospheric SAT scores so you feel forced to make SAT preparation your main extracurricular activity. And they generally charge less money.

If you're willing to limit yourself to the 3,350 out of the nation's 3,500 colleges that don't play the hardball admission game, you can probably skip this entire chapter.

---

[1] This analogy is compliments of the above mentioned Bill Mayher.

INSIDER'S SECRET: There's even a back door into some tough-to-get-into colleges: Get your degree through their night or extension programs—even Harvard offers one. That's a smart option: easier to get into, less expensive, the same or better professors, and the designer label on your diploma. All you miss is the overrated dorm life.

If, however, you insist on the traditional route into the Killer 150, this chapter will show you how to up your chances.

There's a one-minute McVersion of this chapter on pp. 60–61. Be my guest and read just that if you're in a hurry. But realize that if you take that shortcut, you risk getting rejected from all the colleges you apply to. Do you really want to compete against college applicants who took the time to read *all* of your college coach's brilliant yet feasible admission strategies in this chapter? Here they are.

Step 1: Take the Hardest Schedule You Can Without Getting a C in an Academic Subject.

Sounds like fun? Alas, the first thing killer colleges look for is great grades in tough courses. I wish I could tell you that colleges salivate at auto shop, but the fact is, they look for transcripts with five or more academic subjects per term, most of which are honors, Advanced Placement, or International Baccalaureate classes, especially in the 11th and 12th grades. They value these courses so much that they generally prefer a B in an honors class over an A in a regular class, though, of course, they really are happiest with A's in honors courses. Nice of them, huh.

Step 2: Decide Whether to Take the SAT I or ACT, and Whether You Need to Prepare. If You Need to Study, It's Not Worth Going Overboard.

Almost all colleges will accept either the SAT I or ACT, but which should you take?

INSIDER'S SECRET: If you're bright but lazy, try the SAT I. If you're a plugger, have a learning disability, or are weak in math, consider the ACT. Only 25 percent of the ACT is math versus 50 percent on the SAT. Another factor: 25 percent of the ACT is science, and there is no science section on the SAT.

Should you prepare? Take a sample SAT I or ACT under timed conditions. The actual past SATs are commercially available in a book called *10 Real SATs.* For the ACT, actual past exams are available in the book *Getting into the ACT.* And there are other books on the market that will help prepare you for both tests.

Essential truths: If your score on the sample test is in range for your target colleges (check *Profiles of American Colleges* or another of those large college directories, or at *www.usnews.com*), don't waste time preparing. If it's more than 150 points below, consider easier-to-get-into colleges. But if your score is moderately lower (50 to 150 points), here's a smart, easy, and cheap approach to improving your score. Not only will this approach boost your score almost as much as an expensive test prep course, not only will you do it in lots less time, not only will you do it for lots less money, but because of all the time an SAT prep course takes, taking a course can actually lower your school grades. And lower grades hurt you more than extra points on the SAT helps. Here's what to do:

> **Take a sample SAT I or ACT under timed conditions.**

✓ To avoid a low math SAT or ACT score, keep taking math.

✓ Use the free study materials sent to you when you register for the SAT or ACT.

✓ Get a test prep guide. Barron's, The Princeton Review, and Kaplan publish guides for the SAT and ACT in book and CD-ROM formats.

WHEN SHOULD YOU TAKE THE SAT I OR ACT?

Most college counselors tell you to take the exam in May of your junior year. They argue that taking it then gives you an idea of which colleges to consider, and gives you plenty of opportunities to retake. Your college coach disagrees. Unless you're applying Early Decision or Early Action, don't follow the crowds that take it spring of junior year. Take it in October of your senior year. You'll score higher because you've had five more months to mature, and studied during the last weeks of summer vacation. By studying then, it won't cut into your school study time, which could lower your course grades—the #1 factor in college admissions. If you bomb the October exam, there's still time for a retake in December, or even in November if you register within a week after the October exam. Yes, it's helpful to know your approximate SAT score by the spring of your junior year. It can help you decide which colleges are likely to admit you. But you can get an excellent indication from your PSAT score and from your score on a practice exam you can take at home in *10 Real SATs* or *Getting into the ACT*. Of course, take these practice tests under timed conditions.

SHOULD YOU RETAKE THE SAT OR ACT?

Retaking the SAT or ACT rarely results in a big enough increase to significantly improve your college admissibility. You need at least a 60-point increase in the SAT to do that, and according to the latest studies by the College Board, the average increase is 15 to 45 points. And get this—35 percent of repeaters' scores actually go down! More important, time spent studying for the retake often is time taken away from studying for your courses, which can lower your grades, and that can reduce your college admissibility.

BE SMART ABOUT THE SAT II

Most colleges don't require the SAT II, but many of the 150 killer colleges ask you to take three of them. Check each college's application form to be sure, but you're usually safe if you take Writing, Math 1C (or 2C if your PSAT or SAT I is 700+), plus an SAT II of your choice.

INSIDER'S SECRET: It's tough to get a high score on the physics or Chinese exam because top students take it. Easier tests: English literature, biology (ecology option), U.S. history, and Spanish. Prepare using the free booklet you get when you sign up, and if needed, a prep book (Barron's publishes several).

The best time to take SAT IIs is June of your junior year, except for a course that you may have completed at the end of your sophomore year, for example, biology.

SCORE CHOICE: A POOR CHOICE

I want to warn you about *Score Choice*. You're allowed to withhold having one or more SAT II scores sent to colleges until you've seen the results and decide they're good enough. On first glance, that sounds great; you only need to show a score to a college if it's good. But there are problems. Months after the exam, you must member to get the scores released (unlocked from the College Board computer) and—a separate step—to order them sent to each college you're applying to. Many students forget to do one of the steps and end up having no SAT II scores reported, so their college applications end up incomplete. Another problem: If you take an SAT II in your senior year and use *Score Choice*, the scores won't reach the college in time for Early Decision applications or possibly even for some colleges' regular December and January admission deadlines. Even if you use *Score Choice* correctly, it can cost you more than $100 in extra score-reporting fees, and the odds of it affecting whether you'll be admitted to a college, let alone whether you'll be happier and more successful at that college, are tiny. Your college coach doesn't believe *Score Choice* is worth the effort. If, when taking any SAT exam, you know you bombed it, you can simply cancel the score within three days of taking the exam, in which case no record is made of it and you can retake it.

Step 3: Get the College Applications.

Each college's current version is usually available by August or September of your senior year. Just call the admissions office. See p. 16 for things to ask for in addition to the application. Or easier, you can download an application from the college's Web site. More and more colleges even allow you to apply on-line. If you're using pencil-and-paper applications, photocopy the blank form, work on the copy, and only when it's perfect, copy it onto the original. The college will be impressed with how meticulous you are.

TIME-SAVER APPLICATIONS

Imagine applying to as many colleges as you want with just one on-line or print application. Hundreds of the nation's most prominent colleges have agreed to accept one basic application. Companies are fiercely competing to develop the most convenient one and they're evolving rapidly, so rather than recommend a particular one to you now, when you're ready to apply, look at the pros and cons of each of the major players:

The Common Application (*www.commonapp.org,* or 800-253-7746)
CollegeQuest (*www.collegequest.com*)

The companies listed on the next page may, by the time you're reading this, also offer one-size-fits-all applications.

The colleges have signed statements that promise that using these one-size-fits-all applications will *not* hurt a student's chances of admission. Nevertheless, some insiders don't trust the colleges to keep their word. They recommend that—at least for your first-choice college—you complete that college's own application. This isn't necessary if you're applying Early Decision or Early Action.

Another way to ensure that the colleges take your one-size-fits-all application seriously is to, in the "additional information" space, write a paragraph explaining why you're interested in that college.

Even if you want to use the college's own application, there's a shortcut. Three organizations:

the College Board (*www.collegeboard.org*),

CollegeEdge (*www.collegeedge,* 415-778-6262), and

Apply (*www.weapply.com*, 970-346-0336)

offer free on-line or CD-ROM-based software that contains hundreds of colleges' application forms. With either software, you fill in your basic information (name, extracurriculars, etc.) just once. You'll still have to do each college's essay, but you won't have to type in "junior varsity tennis" nine times.

There's usually no extra cost for using any of these special applications. You just pay each college's regular application fee.

Step 4: Make a List of Deadlines.

Think of how miserable you'd feel if after four years of high school coursework, you got rejected from your first-choice college just because you forgot to have your high school transcript or test scores sent to the college on time. It happens, and the college probably won't care if the dog ate it. HINT: Save yourself the grief: On the form on p. 193, write the deadlines for all your colleges. They're listed in the material the colleges will send you and in the one-size-fits-all applications.

TWO TEMPTING BUT RISKY OFFERS FROM THE COLLEGES: EARLY DECISION AND EARLY ACTION

To scoop up the best applicants before other colleges can get 'em and perhaps offer 'em a bigger discount, many four-year colleges offer one of two options—Early Decision or Early Action—that allow you to apply early (usually by November 1 of your senior year) and get your answer early: usually December 15. Both options are risky.

If a college admits you **Early Decision**, you *must* attend that college. Many students change their mind between December and May of their senior year, and if you do, you're stuck unless you find the financial aid award inadequate.

INSIDER'S SECRET: The financial aid package is more likely to be inadequate than if you apply regular decision because the college knows it doesn't have to compete against other colleges' financial aid packages. On the upside, not only do you get to know earlier, your chances of admission are somewhat improved, especially at hard-to-get-into colleges because the college knows you will come if admitted. The edge, however, is modest. Don't be deceived by the statistics that a much higher percentage of early applicants are admitted. A major reason is that the pool of early decision applicants is stronger.

If you decide to apply Early Decision and expect to get financial aid, apply to additional colleges. That way, if your first-choice college offers inadequate financial aid, you can use another college's offer as a bargaining chip or even back out of your Early Decision commitment because of the inadequate aid.

Early Action, offered by a few extremely difficult-to-get-into colleges is also dicey. You don't have to commit to the college until May 1, so you can decide to go elsewhere, and you can apply Early Action to more than one college, but the standards for Early Action admission are usually tougher. Sure you might get a yes earlier, but do you want to pay the price? A bigger risk of getting rejected? And a bigger risk of getting a bad financial aid package?

INSIDER'S SECRET: Early Action can, however, be a useful strategy for students with outstanding records through the junior year, who have completed all their SAT/ACT testing by October, and whose grades are likely to be lower in the senior year.

Except in the above case, your college coach thinks that it's generally smarter to apply regular decision, rather than early. Then in February, write a note to your top-choice college explaining that it is your #1 choice. Colleges want to offer spots to students who are likely to come. The note can simply say, "I just want to let you know that having learned more about the colleges, yours is now my top choice. (Give two to three reasons why.) I'm really hoping you'll admit me."

ONE AWESOME OFFER—FOR THE RIGHT STUDENT

Bored to tears in high school? Feel mature enough to go to college after your junior year? Here's an option that may make sense: Early *Admission*. Many colleges allow exceptional students to begin college after their junior year of high school. One college, Simon's Rock, is exclusively for Early Admission students. To apply for Early Admission, you must apply by May or June of your junior year, and have taken your SAT I or ACT in your junior year.

ARE YOU A HOME-SCHOOLER?

The good news is that most colleges, even famous ones, welcome applications from home-schooled students. The bad news is that because you don't have a standard transcript, you usually must prove that your education was at least as good as a typical high schooler's. And yes, that includes science and math.

So, as early as possible, call the colleges on your list to find out what you'll need to do to impress them. At minimum, you'll probably have to take the General Educational Development (GED) exam. In some states, unless you get a waiver from a school district superintendent, this isn't possible until you're 18 or your high school class graduates; ask your prospective colleges how to handle this. You may also need to take three to five SAT IIs. You'll certainly have to meet your state's high school graduation requirements. If you don't know what they are, contact a counselor at a local public high school or a local home-schooling organization.

Whether required or not, submit a log of all your junior year's educational experiences. Include work samples such as essays and reports of science experiments.

You'll also find these resources helpful: *And What About College*

by Cafi Cohen, *Home Education* magazine;
(*www.home-ed-magazine.com.*) and the Home Schooling Legal
Defense Association Web site: *www.hslda.org.*[1]

Step 5: Complete the Applications.

If you're a procrastinator, hang your list of application deadlines
on the wall or around your neck. Ask your parents to pester you
about them. (Like they won't, anyway!) If pestering you doesn't
work, could it be a sign that you don't want to go straight to college? Should you consider an un-college option? (See p. 201.) A
time-out year? (See p. 37.)

THE PERFECT PARENT: For most students, applying to colleges can be a logistical challenge. This isn't the best time to allow
your child to learn from his mistakes. So, starting in September of
the senior year, if you see that your child isn't making good
progress on the applications on his own, ask your child to post the
chart on p. 193 and every few days, look at the chart together to see
how things are progressing.

INSIDER'S SECRET: Better to list the few extracurriculars you've really focused on than a bunch of quick-
ies like one semester in the chess club, one summer of
football camp, one week of ladling soup to the homeless.
Yes, high school should be time to explore lots of things,
but those spoil-sport killer colleges look for "sustained interest and increased success." For example, they're impressed with the
student who, as a sophomore, wrote for the student newspaper, as a
junior became managing editor, and as a senior, started an alternative
paper.

If you're an athlete, visual or performing artist, or debater, throw
in a tape. If you're a writer, send a sample. If you're a computer
programmer, send your best creation.

How to save a huge amount of time: Don't do an activity just
because it will look good on your application. Unless you're all-star

---

[1] Thanks to Sean Callaway, Director of College Placement at Pace University, for contributing to this section.

caliber, college admissions committees won't care much that you got up at 3 A.M. every day to row on the crew team.

In addition to *the* essay, there are usually short essays like "Why this college?" These are almost as important as the long essay. If you decided to apply to a college by following the steps in Chapters 1 and 2, you'll write a great answer to this question.

Colleges often ask an unfair question: "What other colleges are you applying to?" Your admissibility should depend on your qualifications, not how many colleges you apply to. Colleges want to offer slots to students likely to say yes, but you shouldn't be penalized for making the extra effort to apply to more schools. So, I recommend that you list only one or two colleges.

You have enough to worry about. So, photocopy your completed applications and get a certificate of mailing from the post office to prove you met the deadline. If within a month of mailing, you haven't gotten a postcard from the college stating that it has received your application, just contact the college and offer to send a duplicate application and your certificate of mailing. They'll honor it. Bonus: That photocopy of your college essays and list of extracurriculars and honors may be useful when you apply for summer jobs or scholarships.

DO YOUR ESSAY

Are your parents nagging you to start your college essays? They've clearly forgotten the mental paralysis, the "I don't know what to write" syndrome that has afflicted every college-bound student since the Marquis de Sade invented the college essay.

This eight-step approach works for many essay topics.

1. Think of specific examples from your life that demonstrate how you could benefit the college.

You ask, "How can a teenager benefit Harvard?" Lots of ways. A few examples:

✓ Are you the sort who participates a lot in class? Think of times when you sparked an interesting discussion.

✓ Perhaps you have a personality characteristic that will enhance campus life: Are you enough of a leader to start a skydiving club? Enough of an individualist to start a conservative students club at a liberal school? Compassionate enough to help overwhelmed students? Persistent enough to keep revising your article until it gets published?

✓ Think of specific examples from your life that prove you have such a personality characteristic. If you can't think of any, ask yourself, "If I had to give incoming high school students a speech titled 'What I learned from being a teenager,' what would my main points be?"

✓ Can you excel in an on-campus extracurricular? Could you write an addictive weekly column for the student newspaper? Can you play a mean tuba? Are you compelling enough to get dozens of listeners to call in to your campus radio show? Think of an anecdote from your life that proves it.

✓ Are you unusually well matched to the college?[2] If you're looking for a midsize, highly selective, southern college with a great bio-medical engineering program and you're applying to Duke, you're a great fit.

✓ Would you love to help a prof on his or her research even if your first project is washing 837 test tubes? What in your past can you point to that would prove it?

✓ Would you add diversity to the student body? Are you a coal miner's daughter? Did you grow up in a Pakistani village, or were you a gang member in New York City? What story would bring to life the unusual perspective you would bring to campus?

If you're stuck, ask yourself, "What have I done to improve my high school or my fellow students' experience there?"

Pick a benefit to the college that isn't already apparent from the rest of your application. For example, if you're a varsity athlete or musician or were selected for some special program, you'll have noted those on your list of extracurricular activities or honors, so it would be a waste to write your college essay about that.

---

[2]The main benefit to the college is that a well-matched student is less likely to drop out. Dropouts make the college's statistics look bad and cost it money to recruit another student. Also, a well-matched student is likely to be a happy one and therefore more likely to become an alumni donor.

When in doubt, avoid the following topics. They're used so often that they numb admissions officers. How my visit to another country helped me appreciate another culture, how athletics taught me the importance of hard work or sportsmanship, what I learned from being in student government, and how important my family has been to me.

2. Pick one to four compelling examples that prove you can provide that benefit.

Charlene Liebau, Director of Admissions at Cal Tech, tells of the successful applicant interested in aerospace research. He wrote about the rocket he built in his garage. He planned to launch it, much to the consternation of his parents and neighbors, and to the delight of his friends. But in fact, he blew up the family garage.

Puhleeze, do not do activities just so you can write about them in your college essay. That's prostituting yourself for an advantage that will probably be insignificant in your college admissibility, let alone in improving your career or life prospects. It kills me to see students spend big bucks on some "study trip," or do community service mainly because they think it will look good on their college application. The fact is, these things usually have tiny impacts.

3. Tell each example in one or two paragraphs.

Readers of college essays must try to stay awake through hundreds of oh-so-boring pages, so tell your story vividly and clearly. If you're not a great writer, use simple words and short sentences. The more complicated the writing, the more problems are likely to creep in.

If the essay is sounding artificial, make believe you're writing to your favorite relative. Tone is very important. If it sounds like baloney or is filled with clichés like, "We must celebrate diversity as we face the challenges of the 21st century," you're in trouble. College admissions directors have great hogwash detectors.

4. Write an introduction that hooks 'em.

Use an attention-getting statement or statistic. Here's an introduction with both. "Recently, I read that 85 percent of all high school seniors have been drunk. I'm not surprised."

5. Write a brief conclusion.

One approach is to project into the future. "I plan to continue saying *no* to alcohol, but *yes* to many things. I want to say *yes* to your excellent American history department. I'd like to say *yes* to writing for the *Flat Hat*. I'd even like to say *yes* to lots of parties. But most of all, I want to say *yes* to becoming part of William & Mary's community: top students living and learning together in a beautiful, historic setting. I hope you'll say *yes* to my application."

6. Revise, put it aside, then revise again (and perhaps again).

A week can help you see that your explanation wasn't clear or that your joke was corny.

Read it aloud, one sentence at a time. Check it again for spelling or grammatical errors. Ask yourself, "How can I make this sentence better?" (Clearer? More powerful? In fewer words? More logical?)

Have you conveyed that you're friendly, moderately confident but not boastful, growing not grown, enthusiastic not whining, respectful but not desperate?

> **Don't worry if your essay is not clever—for example, "My life is like a drop of water." Of every ten people who try to be clever or cutesy, nine fail.**

Don't worry if your essay is not clever—for example, "My life is like a drop of water." Of every ten people who try to be clever or cutesy, nine fail. Use the approach that your college coach has just taught you and you may not hit a home run, but you'll be much more likely to hit a single or a double, and that's enough to boost your chances of getting admitted.

7. Get some reviews.

Ask a smart person or two to read it; for example, an English teacher, college counselor, or smart relative. Ask if the points in your essay seem important. Clearly explained? Honest? Does the essay reflect who you are?

8. Make one last revision.

Revise based on your reviewers' feedback. Then read your masterpiece one last time. If you can say, "This is me!" you're done. Congratulations.

Recommendations

Check the box on the recommendation form that "waives confidentiality." That allows the recommender to write the recommendation without your ever seeing it. If you don't waive confidentiality, most colleges will suspect that the recommendation is overly positive.

Choose recommenders who are bright and motivated enough to write a persuasive recommendation. Even if a letter says you're terrific, colleges won't value it much if it sounds like it was written by an airhead. However, colleges will also ignore letters of recommendation from heavy hitters such as politicians, unless they know you well. Alumni who have donated big bucks to the college will almost assuredly not be ignored.

A recommender can often support a contention (look it up—another SAT I word) you make in your application. If you say you want to be a history major, you'll probably want a history teacher as a recommender. If your essay speaks of your inspirational leadership of the football team, ask your coach for a letter. If your essay describes family problems you've overcome, your counselor, therapist, or clergyperson might write a letter.

What makes a recommendation persuasive? Specific examples. How do you get your recommender to include specific examples? Just say, "I'm hoping you might mention X" (for example, "that term paper on antiaging drugs in which I interviewed three scientists"). Also, when giving the form to the recommender, offer your resumé or list of accomplishments.

Your letter of recommendation may not be at the top of your teacher or counselor's to-do list. Unless your school has told you differently, give your recommenders a stamped envelope with the college's address on it, and in the lower left-hand corner, write, "Deadline for mailing: (Insert date)." A few days before the deadline, check back to be sure it will be mailed in time.

Interviewing

Most colleges don't require an interview, and if required, it rarely sways an admission decision. Except for super-hard-to-get-into colleges, an interview is used more to sell you than to judge you. To find out, ask if the interview is *informational* or *evaluative*. Showing up for an on-campus interview can, however, show the admissions office that you're seriously considering the college.

What will you be judged on? Basically, they want to know if you're smart, nice, motivated, and have good values. If most adults like you, you're probably safe. If not, consider not interviewing unless it's required.

Prepare by thinking of a few topics you want to talk about, for example, a powerful experience, a passionate interest. (No, not your girlfriend.)

Have an answer ready for "Why this college?" ("Why not?" isn't good enough.)

Be prepared to discuss a favorite book. (*Teen* magazine doesn't count.)

If there's a reason why you'll probably be a better college student than your high school transcript or test scores suggest, plan on mentioning it.

No need for a jacket and tie, but dress well enough to show that you care. Guys, wear socks. Gals, no tank tops.

IMPORTANT: Realize that the interview is a conversation in which you get to ask questions too. It helps if you go in with a few prepared questions, especially ones that will help you decide whether the college is for you, such as, "What about the college are you most proud of?" Don't be afraid to ask a probing question like, "What's a legitimate gripe that students have about the college?" The interviewer will respect you for being a good consumer. Dorkiest questions: those that are answered in the college catalog or viewbook.

Don't save all of your questions for the end of the interview. Questions are midinterview lifesavers. If you've just given a stupid answer to an incredibly easy question and you're dying to change the topic, try asking one of your questions. (See pp. 26–28 for my favorites.)

Bring your transcript, especially if you'd like to try to explain away weaknesses.

INSIDER'S SECRET

INSIDER'S SECRET: The more powerful the interviewer, the more good an interview can do you. So, especially if you think you'll interview well, ask if you could be interviewed by an associate or assistant director of admissions rather than with an admissions counselor or alum.

Studies have found that you make an extremely hard-to-change impression in the first few seconds you meet someone. How to make a good first impression? It's a sad commentary on human judgment, but all you have to do is follow the advice offered by Gary Ripple, author of *Campus Pursuit*: smile, offer a firm handshake, look the person in the eye, and pleasantly say, "Hi, I'm Bob Jones and these are my parents, Joe and Judy Jones. When should they come back to meet me?" Wait to be invited to sit down, then lean slightly forward, keep a pleasant look on your face (that's pleasant, not psychotic), and maintain eye contact. Believe it or not, in just those few seconds, you're halfway home. The preparation suggested in the previous paragraphs helps ensure the other half.

End using a similar approach. Smile, look the interviewer in the eye, shake his or her hand, and, if true, say that you actually enjoyed the interview. If not, thank him or her for meeting with you.

During the actual interview, be your best self, but be yourself. Interviewers have built-in hogwash detectors.

Frequent mistake: Too short or too long answers. Rule of thumb: Talk for 10–60 seconds, then either ask a question or wait for your interviewer to say something.

INSIDER'S SECRET: Another frequent mistake: Giving a long answer to a hard question to try and come up with something good to say. Instead, remember this rule: short answers to hard questions, longer answers to easy ones. That way, more of the interview will be spent on your strengths, which will leave a better overall impression.

> **Short answers to hard questions, longer answers to easy ones.**

Tips for Athletes and Performers

Ask your coach or teacher if and where you can perform in college. Could you sing for the Yale Whiffenpoofs? For an average college? Or should you confine your singing to the shower?

IMPORTANT: Potential college varsity athletes must follow a special timeline and regulations. See your coach.

Request, if available, a special coded application for potential varsity athletes.

With your application, include a short note to the college coach or artistic director that includes your performance and academic highlights, and a few-minute video of you in action. Artists should send slides. Musicians send a tape. The admissions office will send these materials to the appropriate person for evaluation.

Right after you've applied to the college (an NCAA regulation), ask your coach to phone or write to colleges on your behalf.

For complete advice:*www.ncaa.org/eligibility/cbsa*

If You're Learning Disabled

Mention it on your application. It will probably increase your admissibility at colleges with good support for the disabled and decrease it at schools with minimal support. If you need the help, you don't want to go to low-support colleges anyway.

For more advice, see Marybeth Kravets' and Imy Wax's *K&W Guide to Colleges for the Learning Disabled.*

The McVersion of Chapter 3: How to Get Into Killer Colleges Without Killing Yourself

Here's the 60-second version of this chapter.

✓ The thing that killer colleges most look for? Good grades in tough courses. Take the hardest schedule you can without getting any Cs.

✓ Decide whether you can just walk in and take the SAT I or ACT, or whether you need to prepare. Get a test prep book or CD-ROM that contains sample exams. Take one at home under timed conditions. If your score isn't high enough for your target colleges, consider buying a test prep book or software.

✓ If you're applying to nationally prominent colleges, consider using a one-size-fits-all application such as CollegeEdge (*www.collegeedge.com*), which enables you to apply to as many as you'd like among hundreds of colleges, including many prestigious ones, with a single basic on-line application. Colleges agree to treat a CollegeEdge application the same as their own applications. To be sure a college knows you're serious about attending, in the space provided for "additional information" write a paragraph on "Why this college?"

✓ Enter your college application deadlines on the form on p.193.

✓ For many essay questions, a wise approach is to give examples from your life that demonstrate how you'd benefit the college. For example, discuss the Students Against Drunk Driving chapter you started, the class discussions you've led, or how you were able to get dozens of students to write in to your advice column in the high school newspaper.

✓ Right before an admission interview, read up on the college. Sources: *The Best 311 Colleges*, *The Fiske Guide to Colleges*, *Profiles of American Colleges*, *Barron's Best Buys*, and *Guide to the Most Competitive Colleges*, and the college's admissions publications or Web site. Prepare at least three questions for the interviewer. Ask them during lulls, not just at the end. Be your best self, but be yourself.

✓ If you're wait-listed or rejected from your first-choice college and are sure you'd be much happier there than at any college to which you've been admitted, call or have your counselor call and find out why you weren't admitted. Then submit additional material that might change their mind. Let the college know that if you're admitted (with financial aid?), you will definitely come.

CHAPTER 4
Finding the Money

$4 billion: the increase in Harvard's endowment from 1996–1997.

4.1 percent: the percentage increase in Harvard's tuition from 1996–97.

$2.5 million: the profit Harvard makes each year from MBA application fees alone.

Twenty dollars an hour. I'll bet you wouldn't mind making that. But $20 an hour is nothing compared with what this chapter will probably earn you. The hour you're now about to spend with your college coach will likely net you thousands of dollars.

Your parents are probably going to be paying much of your college expenses, and some of the advice is aimed at them so get at least one parent to read this chapter.

The 60-second McVersion of this chapter is on pp. 79–80, but if you're serious about bagging real bucks, you really should read the whole chapter. As long as you live, this hour may be your best paid of all.

The Most Potent Strategy

The easiest, if most obvious, way to make college affordable is to choose a college with a low sticker price. This is especially true if your family is middle income. Rule of thumb for middle-incomers: If your family income is over $40,000, look first at colleges with an annual cost lower than $17,000. (For the cost of 434 nationally note-worthy colleges, see pp. 165–184.)

Why focus on colleges with a low sticker price? Even after financial aid grants, for four years of college—and remember that many students take five or six—middle-incomers shell out $15,000 to $40,000 *additional in cash* for a high-priced college than for a typical public college. In addition, they're forced to take a $15,000 to $40,000 loan (you have to pay all that back plus interest). And if you don't pay, the government can garnish your salary—and I'm not talking parsley. Why graduate heavily in debt when you can graduate without owing a dime? Your savings could buy a car, wedding, down payment on a house, or more education.

And consider this. With more and more students deciding to go to graduate school, your parents may have to count on paying for college *and* graduate school for each child in your family. Send two kids to a brand-name private college for a bachelor's and master's and we're talking almost $500,000!

You might ask, "At a less expensive college, won't I get an inferior education or have worse career prospects?" Fact is, a college education is one of the few products for which higher cost doesn't necessarily mean better quality. For example, many public colleges are inexpensive, not because they're inferior, but because they're partly paid for by your parents' tax dollars.

> **Fact is, a college education is one of the few products for which higher cost doesn't necessarily mean better quality.**

And regarding career prospects, if private college graduates get better jobs (and that's unclear), it's mainly because, on average, private colleges attract better students to begin with. The Harvard name on a diploma is a big plus, but a Harvard-caliber student at Truman State will probably get great grades, knock-'em-dead recommendations, and the best job leads. So, believe it or not, career-wise, Harvard vs. Truman State is probably a toss-up.

The previous paragraph presumes that you're getting into Harvard. The case for a low-cost public college versus a private college is even stronger if we're talking about the many private colleges that are far less prestigious than Harvard yet cost almost as much.

Private College Traps

Most private colleges, but only a few public ones, will reduce your financial aid if they think your parents can afford to take an additional mortgage to pay for college.

Most private colleges, but only a few public ones, will expect your noncustodial parent to pay. Some even expect parents who have saved well to use money they were planning on for retirement.

In fairness to private colleges, a few fine ones such as those noted in the following section, are inexpensive because they're unusually wealthy and so can afford to keep tuition low. Most other wealthy private colleges, however, such as the Ivys and Stanford, set their sticker price at around $35,000 per year.

Top Values in Higher Education

The few low-cost private colleges. Deep Springs, Rice, Webb Institute of Naval Architecture, Grove City, Cooper Union, Curtis School of Music, Howard, College of the Ozarks, Berea.

Two-year colleges. See pp. 147–149 for an ode to these very underrated institutions.

The U.S. Service Academies. The U.S. Military Academy, the Naval Academy, the Air Force Academy, the Coast Guard Academy, and the Merchant Marine Academy. Tuition is free, but after graduation, there is a four- to five-year commitment to serve as a military officer.

Honors programs at public colleges. Some are listed on p. 185.

Canadian colleges. Heavily subsidized by the government, Canadian colleges are an outstanding value: high quality, low crime. Some hidden treasures: Mt. Allison, Trent, and Acadia are top small colleges; and Queens, McGill, University of Toronto, and University of British Columbia are top universities. Applications for most Canadian colleges are not due until the end of the senior year.

College-within-a-college programs at public colleges. Some are listed on p. 158.

Small public colleges. New College, FL; Mary Washington, VA; St. Mary's, MD; Minnesota-Morris, MN; Truman State, MO; Evergreen, WA; California Maritime Academy, CA; Trenton State, NJ; Cal State Stanislaus, CA; University of North Carolina-Asheville, NC; Ramapo, NJ

Prestige public colleges. William & Mary, University of Virginia, University of Michigan, University of California-Berkeley, University of California-Los Angeles, University of North Carolina-Chapel Hill, Miami University of Ohio

Among public colleges, in-state students pay much lower tuition, usually get more financial aid, and find it easier to be admitted. An ever-dwindling number of public colleges allow out-of-state students who intend to become permanent residents to pay in-state tuition after a year.

Colleges offering a three-year bachelor's. Finish in three years and you not only save a year's college costs, but you're in the job market a year earlier, which may mean an extra $20,000 to $40,000 in your pocket. But you have to be a pretty motivated student to finish in three years. Institutions offering three-year bachelor's degrees include Middlebury, New Hampshire College, Northern Arizona, and Waldorf.

Private colleges—if you're likely to get a lot of financial aid. And who is?

✓ A students applying to colleges that enroll mainly B students

✓ Star athletes

✓ Students from families that earn less than $40,000

✓ African Americans, Hispanics, or Native Americans, especially if their high school record is at least average for that college

Where to Store the Money You're Saving for College

One approach is for your parents to invest in a top-performing, no-load growth mutual fund. A smart bet is one of Vanguard's stock index funds (800-635-1511). A year or two before you need the money, move it to a more stable investment like a Vanguard bond index fund or a CD (Certificate of Deposit).

If having money in growth mutual funds might deprive your parents of sleep, they might consider A to AAA-rated STRIPS (zero-coupon bonds), which promise a fixed rate of return, currently about 5 percent per year.

Many states offer college savings plans, each with pros and cons. The programs change from year to year and from state to state, so your best bet is the so-called 529 Plan, available in a number of states. See at *www.fidelity.com/planning* and compare your state's current deal with the savings strategy outlined here. One thing to watch out for: Most *private* colleges currently view assets in savings plans as the *child's*, which means that each year, 35 percent of that money will be expected to be contributed to college costs. So, unless the rules change, avoid the 529 Plan unless you know that you will be attending a public college or you know you won't be applying for financial aid. (The latter can be a mistake even with a six-figure family income.)

Apply to a Financial Safety College

Apply to what Kal Chany[1] calls a financial safety college—one that is very likely to admit you, whose full sticker price your parents can comfortably afford, and that you'd feel comfortable attending. For middle-incomers, two-year public colleges and four-year instate public colleges are often smart financial safety colleges.

Apply for Financial Aid——Even If Your Family Has Plenty of Bucks

Many colleges require you to apply for financial aid even if you're just interested in a merit-based (how brilliant or talented you are) scholarship or loan. Besides, because the methods for determining financial aid are complex, you just might get need-based aid even if your family has some money tucked away. The only time you should **not** apply for financial aid is if **all** of the following are true:

1. You're dying to go to this college.

2. You seriously doubt you'll be admitted.

3. The college's financial aid materials state that their admissions policy is "need aware." That means that the college is more likely to admit applicants who are willing to pay the full sticker price.

4. Your family can handle the college's sticker price for four years in a row without jeopardizing its financial security.

---

[1] *Paying for College Without Going Broke.* Chany, Kalmon with Geoff Martz. Random House. For those who are very serious about maximizing their financial aid, it's worth consulting that book, Barron's *Complete College Financing Guide* by Marguerite Dennis, or Anna and Robert Leider's *Don't Miss Out.*

To apply for financial aid, each college will ask your parents to complete one or more forms. (See each college's materials for the specifics.) Just by filling out those only moderately excruciating forms, your family will have applied for 90 percent of the available financial aid dollars! And you can even get free help if you get stuck while filling out the most widely required form, the FAFSA (*www.fasa.ed.gov*). Just call 800-4-FED AID, 8 A.M. to 8 P.M. ET, Monday to Friday.

For now, forget about those ads that scream "Send us $75 and you can apply for the six billion dollars of unclaimed scholarships." For most people that's a waste of time and money. (More about that on pp. 72.)

If You're Hoping to Get *Need*-Based Financial Aid

$ **Study hard.** The better your grades and SAT or ACT scores, the more financial aid you're likely to get. This gives a whole new meaning to the advice, "Studying pays."
IMPORTANT! Apply to colleges at which you'll be among the top 25 percent of applicants, and you'll probably get more aid.

$ **Apply to at least four colleges,** especially if some of them have high sticker prices. (See pp. 17–18 to figure out how many you should apply to.) Financial aid awards can vary wildly from college to college, and if your nth-choice college offers you a great deal, you can use that as ammunition for negotiating a better deal from your first-choice college. Or you and your parents may decide that your nth-choice college is offering too good a deal to pass up.

$ **You must meet each college's financial aid deadlines** because the demand for aid exceeds the supply. For Early Decision and Early Action candidates, the deadline is usually in October or November. For regular applicants, many deadlines are only slightly later. Check with each college. Don't forget to sign the forms. More forms are returned to sender for signature than for any other reason.

IMPORTANT: Don't wait to file financial aid forms until your parent does the taxes. Instead, use estimated numbers on the form. If the estimates turn out to be way off, your parent just files the amendment form that everyone automatically gets. Meanwhile, the financial aid form will have been filed by the deadline, and that's what counts.

$ **Don't sound too anxious.** Don't tell the college you're dying to go to it, or worse, apply Early Decision, which locks you into attending that college. Chances are, you'll get less financial aid. Colleges save their financial aid dollars for students they need to entice. A way to show interest without desperation is to let them know in an interview and on your application that the college is "among your top choices."

Okay, my readers, I gotta be honest with you. Although I tried to make the following pages as clear as possible, much of it is still complicated. Worse, it's boring. The good news is that these pages contain keys to saving thousands of dollars. So get up and stretch, take a deep breath, and try to stay with me. I'll make it as simple as possible.

$ **If your parent, brother, or sister has thought about going back to college or grad school, a great time to do it is while you're in college.** If your parent or sibling takes at least six units (usually that's two courses) per term, many colleges will halve your family's expected contribution to college costs! This is often true even if the second college student is attending a low-cost community college! Many private colleges aren't as generous about this.

$ **Money should be saved in your parent's name, not yours.** For some reason, colleges give you much less financial aid if savings are in the student's name. If money is already saved in your name, your family should use that money to pay for your expenses: food, the orthodontist, a car, summer camp, for example. The forms ask for your family's savings as of the day you file the form, so just before the filing date, your parents should prepay taxes, bills, vacations, and so on.

$ You'd think that colleges would encourage students to save money for college. No! After the first $2,200 in earnings (including interest and dividends), colleges subtract 50 cents in financial aid from every

$1 the student earns! So, **starting in January of your junior year of high school, don't earn more than $2,200 in one calendar year, including interest or dividends.** This is a good time to do the volunteer work or unpaid internship you were considering. Of course, do all the paid work you want if your parents are broke and therefore you'll get a lot of aid anyway, or if your parents make too much to qualify for aid. How do you know? This chart estimates the cash your family will be expected to contribute *each year* to college costs. The estimates are based on a parent, age 45, with two kids, one in college. Older parents are expected to pay slightly less. It assumes standard deductions.

> **After the first $2,200 in earnings (including interest and dividends), colleges subtract 50 cents in financial aid from every $1 the student earns!**

HOW MUCH WILL COLLEGES EXPECT YOUR FAMILY TO CONTRIBUTE TO COLLEGE COSTS EACH YEAR?

(An estimate for a family of four)[2]

FAMILY ASSETS[3]	FAMILY'S ADJUSTED GROSS INCOME[4]			
	$30,000	**$60,000**	**$90,000**	**$120,000**
$40,000	$2,000	$8,000	$17,000	$26,000
$90,000	$4,000	$11,000	$20,000	$29,000
$140,000	$6,000	$14,000	$22,000	$32,000

[2] If there are three people in your family, add $1,200. If there are five in your family, subtract $1,200; and for each additional person in your family subtract another $1,200.

[3] Not counting your home equity or savings in a retirement account such as an IRA or 401k.

[4] Before taxes

Most private colleges will expect you to contribute more because they consider your home equity, your noncustodial parent's income, and perhaps your parents' retirement savings.

$ **If your parents have an annual adjusted gross income of under $50,000 and everyone in your family was eligible to file an IRS Form 1040A or 1040EZ (or wasn't required to file a federal income tax return), your financial aid application needn't report family assets, no matter how much your family has!**

$ **Your parents should consider taking capital losses and avoiding capital gains starting January 1 of your junior year in high school through December 31 of your final year of college.** Capital gains are penalized heavily in the financial aid formula.

$ **Your parents should make sure their withholding does not result in a large refund of state income tax.** That will be counted as income in the financial aid formula.

$ **Generous Uncle Albert should not write a check out to you to help pay for college costs.** The more money in a student's account, the less financial aid the college will award. **Uncle Albert should help by writing the actual tuition check or by writing you a check after you graduate from college.** Or try to convince him that the best way to support your college education is to buy you a BMW.

$ **Your parents should try to maximize their contributions to their retirement plans before January 1 of your junior year.**

$ **Take advantage of the government's Hope Scholarship.** If your family has an adjusted gross income of $100,000 or less ($50,000 for single filers) your family can get a tax credit of $1,500 for each of your first two years of college. For the junior and senior years of college, families can claim a tax credit of 20 percent of the first $5,000 of tuition and fees, up to $1,000 per family. And if your family's adjusted gross income is below $75,000 ($55,000 for single filers), you can also deduct up to $1,000 ($2,500 in the year 2001) in college loan interest.

$ **If your family's adjusted gross income _next year_ will be borderline for the Hope Scholarship or Lifetime Learning Credit, Kal Chany suggests that you take steps _this year_ before year-end to minimize your _next year's_ income.** For example, consider taking capital gains and redeeming U.S. Savings Bonds. If you are self-employed, consider postponing business expenses until next year.

$ **If you or your parents own a business, the form will ask for its net worth. Net worth consists only of cash on hand, receivables, furniture, property, and inventory minus accounts payable, debts, and mortgages. It is not the value of the business if your parent were to sell it.** The figures you need are usually found on your parents' company's year-end balance sheet or corporate income tax return. If your parents have assets that could be used for the business, your parents will get more financial aid if they list them as business assets rather than personal assets.

$ **Write a letter to each college's financial aid officer explaining any special circumstances.** For example, your father may have lost his job; your parents are divorcing; your family has unusually high housing, medical, or other costs not asked about on the forms; or your family income is unusually high this year.

$ **If you receive a Stafford loan, you can get better terms by dealing with a local bank that sells its loans to the Student Loan Marketing Association (Sallie Mae.)** To find such a bank, call Sallie Mae at 800-891-1387 or visit its Web site at *www.salliemae.com.*

Consider Applying for the Other 10 Percent of Aid

Earlier in this chapter, I said that you apply for 90 percent of the financial aid dollars by completing just one or two forms. That 90 percent comes from the government and the colleges. The other 10 percent comes from other private sources, like rich Mrs. McGillicuddy or the American Golf Caddies Association. Getting a piece of this 10 percent is likely to depend more on your merit than on your neediness.

Before fantasizing about your private scholarship, listen to this. If you win one of these scholarships, most colleges will reduce your other financial aid. These colleges figure, "Great! This kid got $5,000 from someone else. Now she doesn't need our $5,000."

So, if you're applying for financial aid, it may not be worth all the time and effort to apply for these **private** scholarships (many have long applications and require an essay) unless you are confident you'll win big bucks. You may have reason to be confident if you're an academic star, disabled, an "underrepresented" minority, or if you're applying for a scholarship offered by your parent's employer.

If you're still interested in these private scholarships, know that their deadlines tend to be in the fall, so if you want freshman money, start looking in spring of your junior year of high school. For local scholarships, check at your high school's college counseling office, local Chamber of Commerce or fraternal organizations such as Rotary or American Legion, churches, the military, and especially your parent's employer if it's a large organization. For national scholarships, use a computerized search program. They're available free from

www.scholarships.salliemae.com.

www.collegeboard.org/fundfinder/html/ssrchtop.html

and for America Online users, Keyword *RSP*. Don't have Web access? Phone CASHE at 800-462-2743 to have a questionnaire sent to you. Return the completed questionnaire with $20, and you'll get a list of about two dozen best-fit scholarships.

Most students' efforts to land private scholarships yield less dollars per hour than they could have earned with a job at McDonald's. So if you are going to try for private scholarships, only apply for the handful that seem like the best fits. If, however, you're one of your school's stars or are African American, Hispanic, or Native American, it's worth applying to ten or fifteen.

If you win one of these private scholarships, phone your top-choice colleges: "I've received $X,000 from the Kindness Foundation and I'm checking with each college that admitted me to find out whether that will affect my financial aid." That may pressure the colleges into letting you keep more of your financial aid. For more on negotiating financial aid, see pp.75–76.

If Your Family Needs More Money

Your parents should

$ **consider a home equity loan.** The interest is deductible. Of course, your parents shouldn't take on too much debt or they could lose their home. Then where would you go to do your laundry?

$ **consider a margin loan** (a loan secured by your family's stocks, bonds, or mutual funds). The interest is deductible, and you can deduct the entire amount of the loan from your family assets on the financial aid form. Beware: If the stock market crashes, you may be asked to put up additional stock or cash as security.

$ **Take an unsubsidized Stafford loan, and if necessary, a Plus loan.**
Nearly all colleges offer these to almost any student who applies for financial aid. These loans are ideal for families that don't own a home or don't want to add to their home mortgage. They are unsecured loans, so if you can't pay, you won't lose your home. The interest rate is moderate—currently about 7 percent for Stafford loans, 8 percent for Plus loans. Your college's financial aid office will give you an application.

Other Ways to Cut College Costs

GET COLLEGE CREDIT WITHOUT PAYING TUITION

You can earn as much as a year of college credit, thereby saving a year of tuition, room and board, and get your degree a year faster. How? By taking Advanced Placement or International Baccalaureate courses in high school, and CLEP exams. (See p. 124 for more information.) Be sure your college awards full credit for these toward the college degree.

AMERICORPS

Ready for a break between high school and college? Try Americorps, the National Service Program. Volunteer for a year on such projects as housing renovation, child immunization, or neighborhood policing, and you'll not only recharge your batteries and do good, you'll have earned $4,725 toward education costs, $2,362.50 if you do it part time. For more information, check with:

www.americorps.org

or 800-942-2677.

THE MILITARY

The U.S. Military Academies (Army, Naval, Air Force, and don't forget the Coast Guard and Merchant Marine Academies), offer a quality education, an out-of-classroom experience that some students find extremely rewarding, and a ready-made professional career as a graduation present. And the four-year cost? $0. The hitch? A few-year stint in the military after you graduate college. Phone numbers and Web sites are listed on p. 182.

ROTC. A– grades, 1200 SAT, a varsity letter, and willingness to consider a military career can land you a scholarship that pays all tuition and books, possibly for four years. You'll march on campus, perhaps to the jeers of campus radicals, and commit to two to four years in the military after college. If you're male, you'll be required to get a haircut you'll never forget. Call 800-USA-ROTC (Army), 800-NAV-ROTC (Navy or Marines), 800-423-USAF (Air Force).

HAVE YOUR PARENTS BUY A HOUSE OR CONDO NEAR THE COLLEGE

You live there and rent it to other students. Because all expenses are tax deductible and because good real estate in college towns tends to appreciate, your housing costs could be much less than if you lived in the dorm. You might even make a profit.

After You've Heard from the Colleges

Compare financial aid awards from each college.

✓ How much cash will your family have to come up with? Don't forget about the costs of travel to and from school and the $2,000 to $3,500 a year in living expenses most students incur, for example, for dates, road trips with friends, clothes, and so on.

✓ How big a loan will you have to pay back?

✓ If you applied Early Decision or Early Action, will your award be increased to cover the next year's tuition increase?

✓ As long as your family's income stays the same, will your cash award be renewed each year, or once they gotcha, will they pull the plug?

✓ If, like many students, you take more than four years to graduate, will you get full financial aid in your fifth year? How about the sixth year?

I'm not kidding. Many students do require a sixth year. Imagine that in year six, after all that effort, you couldn't graduate because they pulled the financial aid plug? Find out which colleges won't abandon you.

There's a free on-line service that makes it easy to accurately compare your financial aid awards: *www.usnews.com/usnews/edu/dollars/howtopay/dsawards.htm*

IMPORTANT: If your award from your top-choice college seems too low, negotiate (or better, have your parent negotiate) a better deal with the financial aid office. ***The key is to provide new information that can justify a new decision.*** For example, you might explain that other colleges have offered you a better deal. (Now you see why I want you to apply to at least four colleges?) A tactful approach: "I'd like to attend your college, but I just can't justify spending all that extra money when it would cost so much less to attend College B." Or explain that your family's financial picture isn't as rosy as the financial aid form made it appear. Perhaps your family has big medical expenses, your two siblings will soon be headed for college, or your home badly needs major repairs. Sometimes, sending an itemized budget to the financial aid officer can make your family's situation clearer. Finally, send copies of letters of recommendation from teachers, counselors, coaches, or a boss, explaining what a deserving soul you are.

In College

Once in college, there are lots of things you can do to ease your financial stress level.

LAND YOUR WORK-STUDY JOB

If your financial aid package includes a work-study job, your first stop on campus should be the student employment office. The good jobs go fast. Procrastinate and you may find yourself mopping floors. Some of the most rewarding and scarce jobs are as an assistant to a professor in your prospective major. Ask the department secretary for leads.

Work-study jobs, which are awarded as part of your financial aid package, do not count against you when the college computes your next year's financial aid.

OTHER PART-TIME JOBS

Here are part-time job ideas suggested by Jason Rich in the *Everything College Survival Guide*: tutor (to get clients, put signs on campus bulletin boards); teach students to operate computers; work as a campus representative for a spring break travel organization (check campus bulletin boards); be a mystery shopper (someone hired by national chain stores to visit local stores, pretending to be shoppers, then reporting back to the company on the quality of service they received.) Here are two of the many agencies that hire mystery shoppers: Consumer Opinion Services; 206-241-6050; Imaginus; 716-635-9146.

Remember: If you're getting financial aid, keep your earnings (not counting any work-study job) to less than $2,200 a year because the college will likely reduce your next year's financial aid by 50 percent of what you earned above $2,200.

CHECK YOUR FIRST COLLEGE INVOICE

Be sure your first bill includes all the financial aid they promised you. If not, enter these amounts as a credit and deduct that amount from the total due. Use savings in your own name for tuition.

DEVELOP A BUDGET AND STICK TO IT

Use *Quicken* or Microsoft *Money* software. Or write all your expected expenses in one column, your expected funds in another column. Then write out a plan to keep from overspending. Consult the plan often and stick to it. Very few people can manage this trick, but you're different. Aren't you?

OPEN A CHECKING ACCOUNT

Choose a bank with a branch within walking distance of your dorm room. It should also be convenient to your parents' bank or at least on the same ATM system (Star, Honor, Cirrus, Plus, etc.), so it's easy for them to fatten your account. Of course, keep enough money in your account to cover all the checks you write, plus books, tuition, utilities, weekend road trips, and so on.

As soon as you write a check or make a deposit or withdrawal, write it in the check register that comes with your checkbook. Don't make the classic college student financial move: Write a check for 34 cents. And bounce it.

Save all your banking receipts and compare them with your monthly checking account statement. And hold onto your cancelled checks. They prove you've paid.

THE SECRET TO BEING
A HAPPY CREDIT CARD USER

Especially on credit cards offered to young adults, the interest rate can approach Vito the Shark's. Just remember one thing to stay out of trouble: Charge only as much as you can afford to pay each month. Paying interest gives you no pleasure at all and costs you plenty. And don't be like the 20 percent of college students who carry four or more credit cards. One card—a MasterCard or Visa —will do.

OTHER MONEY SAVERS

$ Watch out for courses with extra fees like lab or photography courses. These can add hundreds of dollars to an already strained budget.

$ If attending an out-of-state public college, you may be wondering if you can qualify for in-state tuition. Probably not. In many states, it used to be easy. Now, most states are clamping down. Nevertheless, it's worth asking the financial aid office how students can qualify for the in-state tuition rate. In a few states, all you may have to do is register your car, vote in that state, and indicate (if it's true) that you plan to live in the state after you graduate.

$ If in midyear, your family's finances change, contact the financial aid office. They have funds available for situations just like that.

$ Most students do their scholarship searching before getting into college. But there is also money for nonfreshmen that may be worth going for. See the financial aid office and the chair of your major department.

Why Is College So Darn Expensive Anyway?

Colleges keep raising tuition. Four years at a brand-name private college costs $140,000. Parents are urged to start saving when Junior is in the sixth grade. Federal aid that is now being given to students simply allows colleges to raise tuition even higher.

Why is no one asking colleges to be more efficient? For example, should professors really be earning a full-time salary for teaching just two or three classes per semester (three classes per *year* at my alma mater, U.C. Berkeley!)? Why aren't interactive, video-based courses taught by the nation's best professors being used instead of large lecture classes? That would raise quality while lowering cost.

The McVersion of Chapter 4: Finding the Money

Here's the 60-second recap of this chapter.

✓ The most potent and easiest (if most obvious) strategy is to attend a college with a low sticker price, usually an in-state public college. If you search carefully using the strategies in Chapter 2, you may be able to get top quality at a public college price.

✓ Even if your parents have built up a nice nest egg, you should probably apply for financial aid.

✓ Colleges have different financial aid forms and deadlines. Be sure you file the right forms, and do it before each college's deadline.

✓ For most families, the smartest approach to saving for college
  is a high-performing, no-load growth mutual fund, for example,
  Vanguard equity index funds (800-635-1511).

✓ Apply to at least four colleges, especially if you're applying to
  expensive ones. The discounts they offer can vary wildly. And you
  can sometimes convince your first-choice college to give you a better
  discount, for example, by showing them the deal that another college
  offered you.

CHAPTER 5

The Keys to a Great College Experience

Sharing a bathroom with 16 strangers, half of them guys? You gotta be kidding!

—Jennifer, Bishop O'Dowd H.S., Oakland, CA.

Ready for the most important statement in this entire book? Here goes: The key to a great college experience is not where you go, it's what you do there. You can have a miserable experience at Harvard and a wonderful one at No-Name State. The good news is that if you handle the 26 decisions in this chapter well, you're almost guaranteed a great college experience. And you'll probably graduate.

Think graduating is no big deal? Think again. In the freshman year alone, 25 percent of students drop out or transfer. And if you were admitted because you're an athlete, child of an alum, or under an affirmative action program, you're at even greater risk. Don't just read this chapter. Study it as if it were the textbook for the most important test you've ever taken. It is.

If you like, don't read about all 26 decisions now. Just flip through the headings and pick one or two timely ones. Then keep this book on your bookshelf at college to be called on as needed.

Your college coach thinks this is the most valuable and most enjoyable chapter in this book. It really will be worth reading every word. But for those of you who insist on the McVersion, it is on pp. 141–143. Here, however, for your dining pleasure, is the gourmet's delight.

I'm Leaving for College Soon. Help!

CRITICAL DECISION #1: WHERE SHOULD I LIVE?

Top Eight Characteristics of On-campus Housing

1. You get to live with lots of other freshmen. It's fun to live with people in the same boat as you are.

2. You live in a cinder-block room so small that it would be illegal to house a welfare recipient there. And you have to share it with another student. Maybe two. And then there's the bathroom you have to share with 19 other freshmen with questionable sanitary habits.

3. It's easier to get involved in campus activities when they're just steps away.

4. Dorm[1] life is a crash course in how to get along with anyone, from cretins to goddesses.

5. It's a good way to make close friends. Often dorm friends move to an off-campus apartment, and have been known, 40 years later, to call each other and reminisce about the good ol' days.

6. There's always something going on in the dorm—a bull session, party, study group—whether you want it or not.

7. Classroom buildings are usually within walking distance. If your college is frozen from December through March, this *will* matter to you.

8. Eating is easy: all-you-can-eat buffets three times a day, and you don't have to lift a finger other than the one holding your fork. Of course, three buffets every day can easily cause the Freshman 10, the typical weight gain. To avoid it, you'll probably need to make friends with salads, fruits and veggies, pasta in marinara sauce, and nonfat frozen yogurt. Don't worry—an occasional hot fudge topping won't turn you into a blimp.

A dorm is not a dorm is not a dorm. A regular dorm, especially one with lots of freshmen, often isn't the "living-learning environment" described in college propaganda. It can be pretty rowdy, and you may find it's hard to study or sleep there. But there are ways to cope with the situation, and you can always move.

You may roll your eyes, but please consider a dorm that attracts nonmaniacs: the quiet, academic, foreign language, honors dorms, and especially living-learning programs (see pp. 151–158). Many students avoid these dorms, envisioning nerd-filled rooms in a monastery-like environment. The truth is that students in these dorms usually have balanced lives: weeknights are generally quiet and weekends are generally social. If you want to find fun, it's

---

[1] The more accurate, if awkward, term is "residence hall."

usually just steps away, but it's nice to be able to count on times when you can study or sleep in your room. Combine the balanced atmosphere with the better students these residence halls attract plus their special extracurricular programming, and it's easy to see how these dorms can be key to a good college experience.

INSIDER'S SECRET: Another key to avoiding unwanted noise is to request a dorm room away from the hall telephone, bathroom, entrance/exit door, or parking lot.

WARNING! Your student housing contract isn't exactly iron-clad. More than a few universities have had problems fulfilling room-and-board promises. Mark Robillard, director of housing at Boston University says, "We don't want to turn people away, but you just can't create beds."[2] Inquiring minds want to know why the heck do colleges admit more students than they can house?

The university sob story doesn't make displaced students feel any better. "We came home and found a guy living in our room's lounge. He was there for two weeks without any notice," says Hofstra freshman Scott Span. Many colleges have turned to hotels and the local YMCA to ease overcrowding.[3]

Top Four Characteristics of Apartment Life

1. No random roommates. You live with whom you want.

2. You have more space for your junk.

3. Costs are higher. Don't forget hidden costs like heating in winter, transportation to campus, and parking, which Worthington and Farrar[4] describe as "the nightmare that never ends."

4. If you live off-campus, it's easy to miss out on the full college experience. You'll have to make extra efforts to get involved in campus activities.

---

[2] *U Magazine*, Sept. 1997

[3] Ibid.

[4] Janet F. Worthington and Ronald T. Farrar, *The Ultimate College Survival Guide* (Princeton, N.J.: Peterson's, 1998). As you'll see, I frequently cite this guide; it's worth a spot on your bookshelf. And these great sites won't even take up any space on your bookshelf: *www.cybercampus.com* and *www.collegeclub.com*.

Top Six Characteristics of Living at Home

1. Your family saves a few thousand bucks each year.

2. You miss out on the intermediate step between the protection of home and the responsibility of living on your own.

3. You may have more spacious surroundings: like your own room plus a living room.

4. You may be able to get home-cooked meals, custom-tailored to your taste.

5. It's easier to do laundry, and it may even be done for you.

6. With fewer distractions and a nagging parent, you may be more likely to get your assignments done.

A Good Compromise

Spend a semester or year in the dorm, then move to a near-campus apartment with a friend or two. If money is a problem and home is nearby, move back home. Or take a job as a live-in nanny or elder companion. Even one term on campus will give you the experience of having gone off to college.

Room with Your Best Friend from High School?

This is usually not a good idea. Of course, you can stay friends, but rooming together too often messes up the friendship or keeps both of you from meeting other people.

CRITICAL DECISION #2: SHOULD I GO TO ORIENTATION?

Don't miss it! It's not just Professor Hassenpfeffer singing the praises of a liberal arts education. Usually, there are activities to help students get to know each other and the campus. For example, a small group of newcomers led by a senior usually explores the campus together and learns how to make the most of the place—everything from how to get football tickets to how to get good profs, from where the jobs are to where the romantic spots are. You'll still be a clueless freshman, but orientation will make you a savvy clueless freshman.

CRITICAL DECISION #3: WHEN SHOULD I SHOW UP ON CAMPUS?

First days can be overwhelming so plan to arrive on campus as early as possible. Ask your roommate to do the same. By meeting each other early, on the off chance you hate each other, there's time for a switch before classes start. While you're on the phone with your roommate, agree about who's going to bring what. No need for two popcorn poppers. See The Special Packing List that follows.

Other advantages of arriving early: the best student jobs go early, more time to meet friends, and you get textbooks before the bookstore line gets out of control.

The Special Packing List
(things that are easy to forget to bring to college)

JUST FOR FUN
- ☐ high school yearbook and other momentos like the trophy you got for bowling a 106
- ☐ photos of your pets and other family members
- ☐ posters, art, anything to cover the walls of your new home
- ☐ stationery and stamps
- ☐ phone/address book, e-mail address book
- ☐ camera
- ☐ your hobby stuff: art supplies, musical instrument. But leave your spider collection home.

ACADEMIC/FINANCIAL
- ☐ cash/traveler's checks
- ☐ quarters for washer/dryer and parking meters (not for video games)

☐ checking account at a bank with ATM service on the same system (Plus, Star, Honor, Cirrus) both near home and on-campus
☐ wallet with your driver's license, social security card, credit card
☐ tuition statements
☐ course registration form
☐ confirmation of admission to the college
☐ housing confirmation
☐ schedule of classes

STUDY STUFF

☐ laptop or subnotebook computer with modem. Great for taking notes in class and for writing papers. Be careful—they're breakable and stolen frequently.
☐ manuals for computer and software
☐ surge suppressor (for your computer, not you)
☐ backup diskettes
☐ printer (don't forget the cable)
☐ desk lamp (halogens give the best light)
☐ scissors, tape, paper clips, stapler, staples
☐ week-at-a-glance pocket calendar—very important (See p. 90)
☐ dictionary
☐ thesaurus
☐ backpack
☐ *The Elements of Style*, a tiny book guaranteed to improve your writing (available at *www.columbia.edu/acis/bartleby/strunk*).
☐ calculator
☐ earplugs (invaluable for studying or sleeping in the dorm)
☐ small tape recorder (Why? See p. 127.)

GENERAL LIVING STUFF

☐ crates to hold books and clothes. Crates double as tables.
☐ fan (for your probably unairconditioned dorm room)
☐ throw rug to provide warm cushiness for your feetsies when you get out of bed
☐ towels

- ☐ wastebasket
- ☐ hangers
- ☐ sewing kit
- ☐ small tool box with the basics: hammer, screwdriver, tape measure, hooks
- ☐ iron, ironing board
- ☐ small vacuum cleaner
- ☐ dishes, mugs, silverware (no, you can't have your family's sterling silver)
- ☐ emergency supply of canned food
- ☐ extension cord and power strip
- ☐ lightbulbs
- ☐ bulletin board and push pins

PERSONAL ITEMS
- ☐ sunglasses
- ☐ sunblock
- ☐ medications
- ☐ first-aid kit, including thermometer
- ☐ bug spray
- ☐ lighted makeup mirror
- ☐ shower bucket with shampoo, soap, flip-flops

CLOTHING

It'll take a year or so for you to perfect your own collegiate look, but a quick peek at the library will clue you in to what students wear at this college. And remember, first weeks at school usually are T-shirt weather. You can have the other stuff shipped later.

"Make each item of clothing earn a spot in your crowded dorm room. Can you see yourself wearing it with at least two outfits?"[5] Pack one to two weeks worth of stuff depending on how often you want to do laundry.

Bring a big robe. It may be a long walk from the shower to your room.

---

[5] Worthington and Farrar, *Ultimate College Survival Guide.*

OTHER MUSTS

- ☐ clock radio or alarm clock (Sorry, wake-up calls are usually not provided.)
- ☐ laundry instructions and fold-up hamper
- ☐ flashlight
- ☐ umbrella
- ☐ answering machine
- ☐ telephone (if not provided by the college)

COOL LUXURIES

Miserly colleges, worried about big electric bills, may nix some of these. Check before schlepping.

- ☐ TV/VCR combination and blank tapes
- ☐ Compact stereo, your favorite music and blank cassette tapes
- ☐ Headphones (to avoid your roommate assassinating you for listening to Smashing Pumpkins while he's trying to study organic chemistry)
- ☐ small fridge (You may prefer to rent one at college.)
- ☐ cooking device (e.g., toaster oven, hot pot, popcorn popper)
- ☐ compact microwave
- ☐ coffee maker
- ☐ full-length mirror

P.S. After packing, if some bedroom or bathroom drawers are still unopened, you probably forgot something.

"Buh-bye Mom and Dad." Now What?

CRITICAL DECISION #4: AM I GOING TO BE SERIOUS ABOUT MANAGING MY TIME?

You're going to be free! Your own boss! You'll decide how you'll spend every minute of every day—whether you like it or not.

Time is your most valuable commodity. So, just for the first few weeks at college until you get into the habit, your college coach really urges you to learn how to make the most of your time. You'll be halfway home to a great college experience.

There are two keys to time management: Having a good system and sticking to it. I'm going to cover both right now.

Keys to Managing Your Time Well

Follow Ben Franklin. Early morning has the fewest distractions. So you'll be able to fit tons more stuff into a day if you can, by any chance—and few young people can—follow old Ben's advice: "Early to bed, early to rise, makes a man healthy, wealthy, and wise." Then again, Ben probably never pulled an all-nighter or rushed a fraternity.

Use a Week-at-a-Glance pocket calendar. Enter everything: due dates for term papers, exams, the basketball game, appointment for meeting with profs, the TV special, your family members' and Sweetie's birthday. For term papers and projects, mark the date you need to start working on them—a good way to prevent No-Doz all-nighters.

Most important, keep a to-do list for every day in your pocket calendar, star the important items, and check it first thing every morning. Make it a habit. Keep it with you all day. As something gets done, cross it off. It will feel good, especially if it's a starred item. As you think of something you need to do, either do it right then or write it down.

Beware of the tube. Martin Spethman, in *How to Get Into and Graduate from College in Four Years*, only half-joking says, "If you never pick up a remote control during college, your chances of graduating in four years double."

Use dead time. There are many bits of dead time during each day—when you're in line, in between classes, on the bus, waiting for a late professor to show up, the ten minutes until *Friends* comes on. If you always keep a book or subnotebook computer with you, you can get hours of work done without giving up a single fun activity.

Take short breaks. Long breaks from studying are big time drains. You can often clear your head quickly with a one-minute break. If that doesn't work, try three minutes. Wanna try a little compulsivity? Set a timer to avoid three minutes turning into 20.

Limit a paying job to 10 to 20 hours a week. Most students can hold a paying job for as many as 10–20 hours a week and still succeed as a full-time student. If you need to work more than 20 hours, see your college's financial aid officer. You may be able to wring a few extra bucks from the college coffers.

These final two suggestions will help you develop a personalized time management system. Each requires a one-time effort, but it will probably be worth it, especially if you have a history of not getting stuff done.

Discover how you really spend your time. For one week, everywhere you go, carry a memo pad and a watch or timer that you can set to go off every 15 minutes. (You can get one for $5 to $10.) Each time it beeps, write what you're doing at that moment. At the end of the week, look over your memo pad. Most students decide to rearrange their priorities.

For example, Mark, a Southwest Missouri State freshman, found that every day he took a ten-minute walk down to the gym to play basketball for a couple of hours. That's 17 hours a week, 17 percent of his waking hours—not counting the shower. He decided that was too much. So, now, most of the time, he rides an exercise bike in his dorm (just a one-minute walk from his room) while reading a textbook 30 minutes every other day, the amount that's supposed to give you maximum benefit for minimal effort. That one change saved Mark 14 hours a week! Plus, he gets some of his studying done.

Take control of your life. Fill in the chart on the next page. Then put it into your pocket calendar *and follow it*. Some people think that following a schedule will restrict your freedom, but it's the opposite. By confining your coursework to your favorite work times, you'll have more time for fun, and those hours won't be spoiled by the guilt of knowing you should be studying.

✓ First, block in your classes (and ideally a few minutes before and after class for reviewing your notes)

✓ recreation time that you know you don't want to give up

✓ exercise (care to try Mark's approach?)

✓ Fill in your prime times for studying (15 to 25 hours a week if you're a typical full-time student). Prime times are the hours that you're fresh enough to concentrate and least likely to be distracted. These prime times are critical. Nothing should pull you away from your desk during prime times—except maybe that great party you're dying to go to.

HOW I SPENT THIS WEEK

	Mon.	Tues.	Weds.	Thurs.	Fri.	Sat.	Sun.
7 A.M.							
8							
9							
10							
11							
12							
1 P.M.							
2							
3							
4							
5							
6							
7							
8							
9							
10							

Now that you have a time-management system, don't let procrastination keep you from using it. Here's how. Actually, let's postpone this part for later. Just kidding.

Cures for the Average Procrastinator

Remind yourself of the benefits of getting the task done. They include higher grades; better writing, reading, and math skills that will help you all your life; not feeling guilty that you didn't get it done.

Think back to times you didn't procrastinate. What were the outcomes? Positive, I'll bet.

Just do it. Do it now, even if you don't feel like it. If you only study when you feel like it, you won't feel like it often enough. Fight the discomfort, and just **do** it. If you're really brave, start with your most difficult assignment first.

Getting started is sometimes the hardest part. So think how great it will feel to have put in a good half-hour. Then literally force yourself to sit down, and **ask yourself, "What is the first tiny thing I have to do?"** For example, "I have to open my assignment book to see what pages I have to read." That can get you rolling.

TRUTH: The more you accomplish, the more you want to accomplish. The less you accomplish, the less you want to accomplish. And it only continues as you get older. You will not wake up when you're 40 and suddenly decide you're willing to work hard.

Be aware of the moment of truth. When you get to that first hard part, I know that it's tempting to sharpen your pencil, grab a Coke, call your girlfriend, or pick your nose. That's the moment you have to force yourself to stay with it (the task, not your nose). **Give yourself a one-second task.** One second is a totally unintimidating amount of time. Often, that one-second task will get you rolling again.

Don't think about how much work you have ahead of you. That can overwhelm you into procrastination. Instead, think like a mountain climber. Just put one foot in front of the other, and when you get to the top and look down, you'll be amazed at how far you've gone.

Only struggle for a minute. After that, get help, decide you can skip it, or come back to it later. Struggling with something for more than a minute usually results in frustration and you end up getting much less done.

Create an artificial deadline. Do you wait until the last minute because you need time pressure to motivate you? Create an artificial deadline. For example, hand your roommate $20. If you don't finish the task by the agreed-on time, she keeps your 20 bucks.

Another approach: give yourself an insanely short amount of time to get an assignment done: "I want to watch *The X-Files* in 30 minutes. Let's see if I can finish all three chapters by then."

Make a deal with yourself. For example, "If I work for two hours, I'll go for a run."

Task seem overwhelming? Like that 30-page term paper on the social, political, and economic variations among the Chinese dynasties? **Draw a thermometer** and tape it to your desk. Instead of numbers on the side, write the little steps you need to do to get the task done. Every time you complete a step, color in that part of the thermometer.

Perfectionism often leads to procrastination. If you feel you must labor over your work until it's perfect, the prospect of work may be such a turnoff that you wait until the last minute, when you simply don't have time to be a perfectionist.

Actually, I'm not asking you to give up your perfectionism. I'm asking you to **defer** your perfectionism. It will make any task much more pleasant. Here's an example. Given a writing assignment, many perfectionists continue to stare at a blank screen until they come up with something really good. That's difficult, so they spend a lot of tortured time staring. Compare that with the productive writer—for example, your college coach, if I may say so myself. I start by typing whatever junk first comes to mind, and keep typing unless an obvious improvement pops into my head. Then after finishing a crummy first draft, I go back and revise (and revise and revise). Revising is infinitely easier than coming up with brilliance out of thin air. Perfectionists can revise as many times as they want, but should defer their perfectionism until the revision stage.

For the Professional Procrastinator

Serious procrastinators feel like a car trying to move with the emergency brake on. Here are some ways to start zooming again.

Hedonism. Some people procrastinate to avoid the pain of work. They forget that procrastination causes much more pain—the ongoing guilt about not having started and the pain that comes from the failures that procrastination causes. The truly hedonistic approach is to get the work done as quickly as reasonably possible, so maximum time is left for pleasure, without any guilt or negative consequences to spoil the fun. Someone once said that procrastination is like a credit card—fun to use, painful when the bill comes in.

Fear of failure. Many serious procrastinators fear failure. Subconsciously they think, "If I don't try, I can't fail." The procrastinator convinces herself, "I could have done it, but I just decided not to try."

The cure is to imagine the worst that could happen if you did fail. Usually it's no big deal. Not trying ensures far greater failure. Not trying is the one thing that *guarantees* failure, the one thing that ensures you'll be perceived as a loser. The fact is, most successful people fail a lot. The difference between winners and losers is how they react to failing. Winners don't waste time on self-pity. They simply learn from their failure so they're more likely to succeed the next time. Even Hall of Fame baseball players have slumps, but they don't sulk. They figure out what bad habit they've gotten into and keep trying to fix it until they're hitting home runs again.

Fear of success. Serious procrastination can also come from the opposite—fear of success: "If I do well here, I'll be expected to do even more in the future."

The cure for this is to keep reminding yourself that you can set limits. There's no need to accept more pressure than you want. For example, many successful executives have decided that the stressful 70-hour weeks aren't worth it no matter how high the salary, and quit and do something low-key such as teaching in college.

Resenting authority. Serious procrastination can come from resenting authority (the professor): "You're not going to make me do that." You're right. No one can make you do anything. But if you make the choice not to do coursework, it's you, not the authority, who will suffer. Ask yourself this: Why am I paying thousands of dollars to do nothing?

If these procrastination cures aren't enough, see if there's a counselor at college who specializes in procrastination, or check if the college offers procrastination workshops. Don't put it off.

THE PERFECT PARENT: If your child is an inveterate procrastinator, ask if he thinks it would be helpful to phone you every day or two to give a progress report. Regular check-in is a key to the success of Weight Watchers and 12-step programs.

CRITICAL DECISION #5: AM I GOING TO GET ALONG WITH MY ROOMMATE?

Worthington and Farrar quote Constance Hays in a *New York Times* essay, who said that the roommate "is at once the most keenly anticipated and deeply feared aspect of the freshman college experience."[6]

It's not easy to get along with your roommate. You may never again have to spend so much time with someone with so few feet of space between you. If they put a welfare recipient in a college

---

[6] Worthington and Farrar, *Ultimate College Survival Guide.*

dorm, the ACLU would probably sue, claiming it's inhumane to make two or three people live in such cramped quarters—and they'd win.

Yet the most helpful advice can be summarized in two words: *be nice.* You're probably nice much of the time naturally. With a roommate you just have to be nice more often. But nice doesn't mean doormat. You and your roommates might want to complete the following document.

Be nice.

ROOMMATE BILL OF RIGHTS

All roommates have the right to

✓ a room that is clean enough. We will define "clean enough" as:

✓ a part of the room that is each person's own. We will separate our room in this way:

✓ expect that roommates will respect personal belongings. Our rule about borrowing will be:

✓ host guests at agreed-on times, with guests respecting the rights of the host, roommates, and other hall residents. The following times are appropriate to host guests:

✓ study free from noise. The following times will be reserved for quiet study:

✓ sleep without noise. Quiet will prevail after the following times:

✓ expect fairness regarding the telephone. Our rule about use of the phone and paying the bill is:

✓ expect that all disagreements will be discussed openly and with respect and that it is acceptable, when any roommate feels it is necessary, to involve a residence hall staff member in the discussion.

We, the undersigned, agree to all of the above. Additionally, we agree that this agreement may be changed by mutual agreement of all roommates.

Signatures:

Date:

But let's be realistic. The likelihood of you and your roommates filling this out and fully sticking to it is about as good as your chances of being named Scholar of the Decade. So remember: Be nice. When "nice" doesn't do it, talk to your roommate about what's bugging you. It's amazing how many conflicts you'll avoid just by saying, "Could you please stop sneaking your dirty clothes into my laundry hamper?" You'll have a better chance of getting your roommate's attention if you preface your request with, "There's something important I want to talk with you about. Is this a good time?"

Even if there is basic agreement, problems will come up. She eavesdropped on your private conversation; he leaves his clothes all over your side of the floor; and so on. Ernest Boyer, in his book *College,* told of a student who said, "I walked in on my roommate when he and his girlfriend were, to put it politely, being passionate on my couch. He had the nerve to get mad at me for 'being so inconsiderate' when I knew he had a guest. "

Bring up your concern, but start with a diplomatic opening line such as, "I hope this isn't a stupid question," "Please forgive me for asking," or "I need a big favor."

Remember, though, what Tolstoy said, "Everyone thinks of changing humanity. No one thinks of changing themselves."

Everyone messes up occasionally, but what if despite repeated tactful reminders and compromising, your roommate and you can't work things out? Remember, you're paying good money to attend this college, and that entitles you to a reasonable roommate. Speak with your resident assistant, the older student who is paid to live in your dorm to handle problems like this. If that doesn't fix the problem, insist on a new roommate, or move.

You can increase your odds of being happy with your roommate by being really honest when completing the roommate-matching questionnaire that you'll receive when first admitted to college. If you are an incorrigible partier, don't say you're quiet just because it sounds better.

What Am I Going to Do for Fun?

CRITICAL DECISION #6: WILL I MAKE FRIENDS?

It can be scary. Away from home for four whole years! What if you don't make friends? What if you're so lonely that you call home twice a day? What if you end up spending every spare moment watching stupid TV shows because there's no one to do anything with?

Not to worry. You'll be around thousands of other students eager to meet new people, and you'll have endless opportunities to meet them: classes, games, parties, exercising, lines, meals, and so on.

But you say you want an extra measure of security? No problem. You've come to the right place. Your college coach interviewed dozens of students who made lots of friends to discover the secrets to their success. Now those secrets are yours. Laurie's story summarized what I learned:

> I know how to make friends because my Army family relocated so often. I was kind of nervous when I arrived at college, but I knew that all the other freshmen probably were too, so I immediately started conversations with just about anyone who looked nice. I met them in all sorts of places—in class (I made a point of showing up a few minutes early), in one of those lines you're always in at college, in the dining hall, at the chemistry majors club, in the orchestra (which I immediately joined—a great place to meet people), at a student mixer in the dorm, in the library (a very cute guy I made sure to sit across from), on the jogging trail, in the student union, during intramural volleyball, in the laundry room. The laundry room is a great place to meet people—you've got nothing to do but talk for a half hour.
>
> You'd be amazed how approachable people are, even the gorgeous

ones. Most people are mirrors—if you notice they aren't smiling or being friendly to you, they're probably responding to the way you're acting. Smile!

Don't wait for someone to start talking to you. You can start a conversation by talking about almost anything: "Gee, this is a long line." "That was an interesting class." "You a freshman, too?" "How's the burrito?"

Once the conversation started, I tried to really listen well and then ask a follow-up question or comment that built on what they said. I might ask about their classes, where they're from, what made them choose this college, the dorm, their family, or what activities they do in college. If I wanted to develop a friendship, next I'd say, "Hey maybe we can get together sometime. Can I have your phone number?" Then I'd phone and say something like, "Listen, I gotta do my laundry. Wanna keep me company?" or "I've had enough studying. Wanna go down to the snack bar?" Right before school started, I threw a back-to-the-grind party and invited my entire dorm floor. Pretty soon, I had a nice network of friends."

Of course, making friends is too complicated to be reduced to a formula, but someone who has just arrived at college may not know where to begin. Laurie's way, the way recommended by the popular students surveyed by your college coach, can help ensure you won't spend four years in solitary confinement.

Laurie was pretty assertive. But what if you're shy? Worthington and Farrar offer this advice: Leave your dorm room door open and keep music on. Read the campus newspaper every day and look for interesting upcoming events and meetings. (And go!) If you're feeling left out, drop in on your dorm's resident advisor or make an appointment to see a counselor at the student counseling center. Many college students feel sad at times, and college counselors have lots of experience in helping.

No matter what your approach, start early. Those first few weeks are when everyone is looking to meet people. If you lock yourself up in your room waiting for someone to drop in, you'll blow a great chance at a social life, and your dorm neighbors might think you're stuck up or want to be left alone.[7]

Use these tips and your phone calls to Mom and Dad will probably be to tell them about the great time you're having.

---

[7] Worthington and Farrar, *Ultimate College Survival Guide.*

CRITICAL DECISION #7: WHO WILL BE MY CLOSE FRIENDS?

This is impossible to reduce to a few words, but consider this. Choose friends who help you to be your best self, not those who seem disappointed by your success or try to drag you down with them. If they give you more anxiety than energy, look elsewhere. Of course, you, too, should try to help your friends be their best selves.

CRITICAL DECISION #8: WILL I HAVE A GOOD ROMANTIC LIFE?

"First of all, lighten up...Don't look at everyone as a potential girlfriend or boyfriend, and don't think of every person you date as your future mate for life."[8] College really is a good time to make friends with and date a number of people. When it's time, the right one will drop out of the sky. Think that, anyway.

And women, do you like a guy? Don't wait helplessly like the passive females of the '50s. Ask him out, if you want.

> Go out in groups...That lets you see how he acts around other people. If he is a jerk, this might be more obvious when you're sitting around a table with six other people having pizza than when you're making out in someone's dorm room...If you're going to become serious, do it slowly. Get to know each other in safe, casual settings.
>
> Find cheap ways to have fun...Don't get stuck on the idea of dazzling your dates; charming them is less important than just communicating with them...Make it an adventure: "Hey, I've got a coupon for a free dessert at Cappuccino Cafe. Want to go"?[9]

Dates on $10 or Less

Here are some freebie/cheapie date ideas from Worthington and Farrar plus some that your college coach thinks are cool.

✓ Attend a play or concert rehearsal (often more interesting than the concert).

---

[8] Ibid.
[9] Ibid

✓ Read aloud to each other, maybe poetry or a play.

✓ Dress up with your partner and enjoy a formal dinner at home with good food and wine.

✓ Explore a city as a tourist would.

✓ Cheer on the varsity. Don't forget about less common sports.

✓ See what's going on at the college: rally, concert, play, movie, lecture?

✓ Drive the back roads just to enjoy the scenery.

✓ Play cards for pennies, not dollars.

✓ Attend a free concert in the park.

✓ Make a coffee date or breakfast date to start the morning.

✓ Visit friends in a nearby city.

✓ Have a snowball fight.

✓ Volunteer for a day.

✓ Hear a lecture or concert at the local museum.

✓ Play a board game like Monopoly; have popcorn.

✓ See a movie in the afternoon before the prices go up.

✓ Browse around a local shopping center.

✓ See if there are "rush" tickets for last-minute theatergoers.

✓ Play tennis or ping-pong.

✓ Go camping or backpacking.

✓ Support your local campus artists by attending a showing.

✓ Fly a kite in the park.

✓ Have a picnic at a quiet spot.

✓ Row a boat on the lake.

✓ Play miniature golf.

✓ Hike through a nearby forest.

✓ Attend a reading at a bookstore.

✓ Try canoeing or rock climbing.

✓ Spend an afternoon at the beach or park. Collect shells or leaves.

✓ Visit the zoo and feed the animals.

More advice from Worthington and Farrar: Go Dutch. The ancient tradition of guys paying for everything is bad for everyone. The guy is unfairly stuck with all the costs, which makes the girl feel like she has to pay him back in one way or another. Either split the check, or agree that you'll pay on one date, she'll pay the next time. Work out the details in advance so you avoid a mood-dampening discussion over who picks up the check.

Hint: Be sure you've brushed your teeth and used deodorant. Sounds obvious, but I've heard enough tales of dragon breath and locker-room B.O. to mention this.

Hometown Honeys

It may be tough to deal with your boy/girlfriend from high school. If it's someone you'd like to keep in contact with, reassure him or her that you can, but it's great to go out with others. If it was meant to be, you'll feel even surer about each other after you've both dated other people.

Avoiding AIDS and Other Nasties

Abstinence ain't bad. Plenty of intimacy and fun is possible without the risk of AIDS, other sexually transmitted diseases, and, of course, pregnancy.

If you do choose to have intercourse, a strict "no glove, no love" policy is the best way to minimize the risks that go along with sex. Condoms pack a one-two punch, preventing both STD's and unwanted pregnancies. You're in college, which presumably means you're smart, so don't make a stupid mistake that could change the rest of your life. Even if you've been with someone for months and have been tested, condoms are still a good idea.

Many guys hate wearing condoms. Under the influence of alcohol or drugs, even many nice guys will downplay the risk to avoid having to wear one. Besides, he may not know that one of his previous partners slept with someone who is HIV positive. You're not just having sex with your partner; you're sleeping with every other person your partner has ever slept with.

Avoiding Date Rape

A word to girls: If you're not sure you can trust your partner, and especially if either of you is under the influence, don't be in a private place. And if you've been dumb enough to ignore that advice, and you mean NO, you must make it plain. That means, when he goes too far, you stand up, and in a strong voice, say,

> **Many guys interpret a half-hearted "no" while you're still lying there as "Convince me."**

"I'm sorry, but no." (This is tough if you're under the influence.) Many guys interpret a half-hearted "no" while you're still lying there as "Convince me." If you mean "maybe," don't say no. He's not a mind reader. If you give an unclear message, it's probably unfair of you to yell "date rape" the next morning.

A word to guys: Neanderthal days are over. Push yourself where you're not wanted, and not only are you being unfair, every woman will soon think of you as "that jerk." Women talk with each other. A lot. If she wants you, she will, at least in nonverbal ways, let you know. Besides, the legal tables have turned. On many college campuses, right or wrong, if a woman charges date rape or sexual harassment, you're often presumed guilty until proven innocent. Unfair but true.

CRITICAL DECISION #9: SHOULD I WALK ALONE AT NIGHT?

Especially if your campus is in a high-crime area, and especially at night, use the campus escort service, or at least don't walk alone. If you're accosted, yell at the top of your lungs, "Fire!" That's the word most likely to attract a Good Samaritan. That white lie is unlikely to put your savior in danger. Just the sight of another person is usually enough to make the perpetrator flee.

CRITICAL DECISION #10: HOW CLOSE SHOULD I STAY WITH MY PARENTS AND HIGH SCHOOL FRIENDS?

For the next few years, college will be your home, but "it would be unusual—in fact, downright strange and insulting to your family—if you didn't feel minor or even major homesickness. Be glad you come from a home that's good enough to miss. This will get better over time."[10] Phoning home or visiting on weekends doesn't make you a baby—especially if the visit includes free laundry, a shopping spree, or extra cash.

The same goes for high school friends. Keep in touch until you outgrow each other.

And while we're talking about high school, think back to what you did there to make yourself feel comfortable. How did you find friends? What did you get involved in? Perhaps what worked for you in high school will work in college.

Another antidote to homesickness is parents' weekend. (Make hotel reservations for your parents very early. They fill up fast.) If your college doesn't have a parents' weekend, Worthington and Farrar suggest that you create one. Invite your parents for the weekend and schedule things for them to do that will make them (and you) feel good about the college.

In addition to providing TLC, parents are a great source of advice because they know you and probably care about you more than anyone else. And believe it or not, they actually were teenagers themselves. Even if you feel you don't need their advice, hear it without feeling that you're being invaded. Your parents are learning how to live with less control over you. It's hard.

Perhaps *the* sign of maturity is to actually ask for your parents' suggestions and to listen to their unsolicited advice. I didn't say you must follow their advice. Just treat your parents' advice as if it

---

[10] Ibid.

came from a caring friend. Accept or reject it on its merits. Only immature people reject advice just because it comes from their parents.

Remember: Your parents are also going through an ordeal. Instead of freshman year, it's the empty-nest syndrome, and they might have difficulty letting go or getting used to a quiet house. Go easy on them—call, write, and e-mail them to keep them updated on school, your life, new friends. That'll keep them from calling every other day or leaving those long, pathetic messages on your answer machine.

CRITICAL DECISION #11: "HEY, WANNA GET WASTED?"

I can hear you thinking, "Oh no. Not another lecture about drinking and drugs!" Sorry, but I couldn't feel good about writing a college guide without saying something about it.

Why? Because the most depressing thing I've found in my years of working with college and college-bound students is how, even at prestigious colleges, many students waste away their college years and may even mess up their entire lives because of alcohol or drugs. For them, college is the world's most expensive cover charge. Thousands of college students say, "I can handle it," and by the time they realize they can't, it's too late. So, I feel compelled to tell you a little of what I've learned from talking with lots of students.

It's not surprising that students drink or smoke marijuana at college. Alcohol or pot may provide a way to relax, feel cool, and avoid being judged as if you were on your best behavior. And the booze companies spend millions to brainwash you into thinking that alcohol unlocks the door to happiness. But picture having a gallon of beer sloshing around in you. Imagine other students looking at you sitting there stoned and thinking what a loser you are.

These visions appeal to few students, yet some get stoned or drunk every week or even more. Especially if they hang out with other losers, it's easy to drink or smoke away four years of social life without realizing what they've done. If they graduate, they will have made worse friends and missed out on the best parts of college life.

This is not a plea for abstinence. It's a request for conscious choice. I know it's hard to set a limit, but try to—in advance—decide if and approximately how much you want to drink. Unless you have an addictive personality, there's nothing wrong with a drink or two (if it's legal) to take the edge off or to quell a bit of nervousness at a party. But much more than that can reduce your social life to hovering over a toilet, acting like an ass, or passing out and missing the fun. It can turn you into a permanent loser and maybe even cost you your life in a car accident.

It goes without saying that drinking and driving is beyond stupid, let alone riding with someone who has been drinking. Get a cab or remember to assign a designated driver—someone who agrees not to drink for the night *and* sticks to the agreement. Also, many campuses have safe-ride programs.

There's good news. "You may be pleasantly surprised to find out that there is less peer pressure to drink or do drugs in college than there was in high school. If you just tell the truth and say you'd rather have a Coke, it's probably not going to matter to most people."[11]

You won't have a problem if you stay away from people who frequently get drunk and from parties where the main objective is to get loaded. Do you really want to be friends with them anyway? Is getting plastered really fun? At a party, hang out with the unstoned. They may not be as obvious as the big boozers, but most parties have them, and they do have fun. Some camouflage themselves by nursing a beer for an hour or sipping a faux gin and tonic: sparkling water with a slice of lime.

Here's a tip: An easy way to say no is to volunteer to be the designated driver.

---

[11] Worthington and Farrar, *Ultimate College Survival Guide.*

Are you abusing alcohol? Try this test:

✓ Do you ever crave, not just desire, alcohol?

✓ At a party, do you often get drunk?

✓ Do you usually have more than one or two drinks in an evening?

✓ Do you ever drink before going to class?

✓ Have family or friends commented about how much alcohol you consume?

If you answered yes to even one of these questions you probably have a drinking problem.[12] If you're concerned about alcohol or drug abuse, choose an alcohol- and drug-free dorm, or join a campus student group such as B.A.C.C.H.U.S. or Students Against Drunk Driving (S.A.D.D.). If you already have a problem, join Alcoholics

> **Here's a tip: An easy way to say no is to volunteer to be the designated driver.**

Anonymous (look in the phone book for a nearby location).

With drugs, you really should just say no. Drugs are unregulated, so you can't be sure what they put into that pot: PCP, paraquat, all sorts of stuff that can toast your brain. And it has become clear that long-term use of marijuana will lower your brain power and motivation. Stronger drugs are like Russian roulette, but fortunately not many students are that crazy, so we won't talk about that poison here. In addition, they are illegal.

THE PERFECT PARENT: While this is a personal decision, in general, parents may be wise to take a moderate approach. If you insist on absolute abstinence from drinking, drugs, or sex, you increase the risk of your child rebelling once he's away from your watchful eye. However, if you wink at getting drunk or stoned, you also increase your child's likelihood of abuse. What often works best is a message that says something like, "Your decision to occasionally use alcohol or pot or not to is a personal one. If you decide not to,

PERFECT
PARENTS

---

[12] Jason Rich, *The Everything College Survival Book.* (Holbrook, MA: Adams Media, 1997).

terrific. If you decide to do it, I would only ask that you consider being moderate, and to not drive while under the influence."

CRITICAL DECISION #12: AM I GOING TO SMOKE CIGARETTES?

Tobacco companies seduce millions of teenagers into smoking, even though the corporations know it will kill half of those teens, most of them to cancer, probably *the* most painful way to die. Do you really want to let those truly evil people do that to you?

According to a government report, half of smokers who began when they were teenagers will eventually die from it, probably prematurely in middle age. That cuts 20 to 25 years from your life expectancy! Think about it, dying 20 to 25 years sooner? And for what? So you can turn off your friends because your breath and clothes stink? So you can enjoy the benefits of yellow teeth? So you can't taste food as well? So your babies have a greater chance of being born deformed? Oh, and let's not forget about the money. Smoke a pack a day and we're talking almost $1,000 each and every year! Can you possibly think of anything you could spend $1,000 on that doesn't have the above liabilities?

Yeah, I can hear you say, "but smoking is cool." What would you say if your twin said she smoked because it was cool? Or because it calms her down? Or what if your twin said, "It's OK. I can stop whenever I want."

Are you already addicted? See if your college's health center offers smoke-enders groups. Or call 1-800-4-CANCER. Better to call them now for information on ways to stop smoking than to call them later to find out about chemotherapy to treat your cancer.

CRITICAL DECISION #13: WHAT ACTIVITIES AM I GOING TO GET INVOLVED IN?

A Carnegie Foundation study found that only 36 percent of college students participate in student activities other than sports. When I show graduates a list of extracurriculars offered at their college, the most frequent response is, "Gee, I would have done that if I had known it was available." So, if you think you might like to get involved in a campus activity, get the list of your college's clubs and organizations. It's usually in the catalog or in a booklet available at your college's student union or office of student activities. Because many students never see this list, some colleges run activities fairs at which representatives of dozens of student organizations sit at tables answering questions. Check out a few organizations and you'll probably find at least one that fits. And don't forget about campus bulletin boards and the student newspaper. They're more likely to clue you in on adventurous opportunities not listed in official college publications.

> **When I show graduates a list of extracurriculars offered at their college, the most frequent response is, "Gee, I would have done that if I had known it was available."**

Get Mentored, Then Become a Mentor

Most campuses offer a junior or senior mentor to freshmen, especially to minorities. Mentoring is rewarding both for the mentor and the protege. There's nothing like a one-on-one relationship.

Clubs

Every college has dozens of student clubs, and if none suits you, most colleges will help you start your own.

INSIDER'S SECRET: Leadership positions, which can help you prepare for later success, often go unfilled. For example, I heard that at St. Mary's College of Maryland, there was a frantic search for a yearbook editor just before work on it had to begin. On every campus, there are student organizations without a strong leader. These are opportunities just waiting to be taken. Students in these positions often get to participate in a campus leadership program that teaches them public speaking, how to effect change, and how to develop confidence—things that, in the long run, may help you more than most courses.

Clubs affiliated with your major are often more interesting than you might think. A biology majors' club might include a field trip to see gene splicing at a biotech company, a seminar on careers in genetics followed by a party, or a talk on bioethics followed by a softball game. These clubs give you the chance to meet students with a common interest. You find out the courses and professors to take and those to avoid. You get to meet dedicated professors on an informal basis, which can yield good advice, a mentor, and research opportunities. Many students find that joining a major-affiliated club even increases their interest in their major, which makes it easier to study.

Student Government

Student governments usually decide how to spend many thousands of dollars, and advise administration on everything from affirmative action to entertainment. You don't need to win an election to get involved. Student government has many committees that need members, even chairs. (Not the kind you sit in, silly.) Many positions go vacant because students don't know about them. Leadership opportunities are also available in residence hall government.

Campuswide Committees

At many colleges, there are student members on the faculty senate, the president's roundtable, and so on. At Queens College, students make up one-third of the academic senate. These committees plan student activities, establish campuswide policies, and select award winners. If you're interested, talk with someone in the office of student affairs.

Honors Program

As discussed on pp. 152–153, this often enables you to have an Ivy experience at a regular ol' college.

Service Organizations

These groups do good works such as helping the elderly or illiterate. Often members of a service organization get together for parties and other social events. Many campuses have a clearinghouse of community service opportunities. Others have a chapter of Alpha Phi Omega, a fraternity that emphasizes service.

State or Nationwide Professional Organizations

Such organizations exist for majors in most fields, for example, the American Psychological Association. They often have local chapters and annual state and national conventions, which allow you to rub elbows with active professionals and students in your field from around the nation. Grad schools like to see these on your application, especially if you presented a paper.

Student Newspaper

Here, you can hone your writing skills and hang out with some of the campus's more outspoken students. Working on the newspaper can also make you feel like you're really making a difference.

Radio Station

From working as a DJ to doing promotions, campus radio station gigs are fun and may even pave the way to a future career. The news department is often a particularly interesting place to work.

Intercollegiate Sports

Even though I was a benchwarmer, I loved playing baseball in college. But if you're thinking that varsity play could be a ticket to the pros, remember that unless you're a high school All-American who will be *the* star on a NCAA Division I top-25 team, you have a better chance of being named president of the college. (See p. 199 for more details.)

Making Connections

Even if you're not particularly interested in making career-boosting connections, it's fun to see how the other half lives. Consider extracurriculars that tend to attract the wealthy and well-connected.

- ✓ golf, tennis, sailing, rugby, fencing, lacrosse, or crew teams
- ✓ fraternities or sororities
- ✓ formal dances on campus
- ✓ expensive on-campus housing
- ✓ expensive university-sponsored recreation

✓ the student arm of the alumni association (alums who are active in the alumni association often have successful careers). Many colleges encourage students to help alumni to plan activities such as homecoming and parents' weekend. If your school's alumni association doesn't have a student arm, see if students are allowed to join the regular alumni association.

THE PERFECT PARENT: During the first week of college, ask if your child has looked into any extracurricular activities. If not, ask your child to consider visiting the student activities office to get the master list.

CRITICAL DECISION #14: SHOULD I GO GREEK?

At their best, fraternities and sororities offer a lot. They provide a built-in social life. They can offer lasting friendships and career connections. Greeks play an active role in campus social life and traditions such as homecoming, which can make you feel like you're a part of history. Many Greek organizations do considerable community service, for example, "adopting" home-bound senior citizens. Greek organizations also provide exceptional leadership opportunities within the house and in campuswide government, because Greek organizations often vote as a block. It's not unusual for half of the student government to be Greek, although fewer than 10 percent of the student body are members.

All these opportunities may explain why a *Fortune* magazine study found that more than 70 percent of the officers of the 750 largest United States corporations who went to colleges with Greek organizations belong to them. The majority of U.S. senators are Greeks, as are Jane Pauley, Ronald Reagan, David Letterman, and Ted Koppel, to name a few.

Contrary to the stereotype, Greek organizations can even help your grades. Many houses have mandatory study hours, in-house study buddies, and old test files; and they boast grades at or above the campuswide average. Until a few years ago, the black fraternity Alpha Kappa Alpha, with alumni such as Martin Luther King, Jr. and Thurgood Marshall, used to paddle students whose grades weren't high enough.

Some fraternities and sororities are deemphasizing the role of alcohol, for example, by having dry rushes, and eschewing kegs in favor of bring-your-own-cans.

Unfortunately, many fraternities and sororities are not like this. Pledging can mean six months of slavery: "Hey, pledge, clean up after the party! I don't care about your econ final. You should have studied earlier, boy!"

Even after you're a member, some houses aren't overly concerned about coursework. Your grades won't be helped by living in a fraternity that schedules Cowboy Night during finals week. At some fraternities, the *typical* member drinks a gallon of beer in a night, at least once a week. And here is a statistic so shocking I can't even believe it: according to an Associated Press report that was cited in *Time* magazine, 86 percent of fraternity residents "are presumed to be binge drinkers."

At some houses, brothers and sisters are enthusiastic about their communal rights—like the right to your deodorant—but not so enthusiastic about their communal responsibilities—like keeping the house clean. Some members, looking back after college graduation, felt that Greek life forced them to spend too much time on silly rituals and traditions, expected participation in intramural sports, had too many parties,

> **Clearly, not all Greek-letter organizations are alike, so be a good shopper.**

was a culture that reinforced gender stereotypes, and caused them to interact primarily with look-alike/act-alike/think-alike people. And it can get expensive.

Clearly, not all Greek-letter organizations are alike, so be a good shopper. Rush week is when you and the Greek organizations check each other out. Are they right for you, are you right for them?

Before you get bombarded by the sales pitches during rush week, speak with an unbiased source: an officer on the Interfraternity or Panhellenic Council or the college sponsor. These people often have lots of information on each house (for example, grade point average, the number of complaints lodged against it, how much it raised for charity). They know which are *Animal Houses*, which require a designer wardrobe, and which subject pledges to harassment. Tom Dougan, Executive Officer of Student Affairs at the University of Rhode Island, said, "I love when students call about fraternities and sororities. I give them the straight scoop."

Hazing is the harassment and ridicule of pledges. University of Texas freshman Mark Seeberger was forced to consume 18 ounces of rum within two hours—giving him a blood alcohol content of .43. (A person is legally drunk at .05–.10.) Seeberger was then dropped off in a rural location and forced to find his way home. He never made it. This absurd practice now occurs only at some houses. Do you really want to join a fraternity or sorority in which your worth is determined by how much punishment you're willing to take?

Here are some more tips on whether to go Greek.

✓ Don't "suicide," that is, rush only one house. Its members may not be as crazy about you as you are about them.

✓ Don't rely on reputation. Tappa Nu Keg may have developed its good reputation based on the national fraternity, not the local, or on past years' members, not the current crop.

✓ Will you have to conform to a narrow set of values? College is supposed to broaden your perspective. Some Greek houses narrow it.

✓ Don't decide based on a party. Visit the house on a typical weeknight and weekend day. Ask questions such as:

How's your fraternity or sorority different from others?
Describe your pledging process. What will you expect from me?
What can I expect from your chapter?
After I'm a member, in a typical week, how much time will I be asked to devote to I Phelta Thi?
How much should I budget for a year in your fraternity or sorority?
How big a role does sports play in your fraternity? Charity work?

What costs are involved in membership? What "extras" inevitably come up (for example, buying presents for big brothers/sisters, purchasing photos at the weekly dance, "must" ski trips)?

Sure, a few houses may reject you for asking these questions, but that's fine. You want a house where someone who asks intelligent questions is welcomed, not ridiculed. This may sound corny, but it's important: Be yourself when you rush. Phoniness may land you a bid, but once in, you'll have to keep up the act for four years or risk becoming an outcast. If a fraternity or sorority doesn't want the real you, you don't want it. There are many other social groups on campus, from choral clubs to karate clubs, that will accept you for who you are. On the other hand, if you are wondering why you were rejected, it may be valuable to ask for feedback.

Oh Yeah, Academics

Students are happy when classes are cancelled.
That makes college the only purchase that people
*are happy with when they **don't** get what they paid for...*
—Newt Gingrich

CRITICAL DECISION #15: SHOULD I SEEK OUT PROFESSORS?

You'll probably grow as much from your one-on-one relationships as from your classes. We've already talked about how to develop good one-on-one relationships with students. Here we'll talk about professors.

Your First One-on-One with a Prof: Your Advisor

You'll probably be assigned an advisor, usually a professor in your prospective major. My daughter had heard about a wonderful professor, Jennifer Wilson, and requested her as an advisor. That turned out to be key to her college experience.

If you're lucky, your advisor will not only know what courses you have to take, she'll recommend great profs; help you plan a program that gets you a good education without overloading your schedule; ensure that you don't find out three days before you expect to graduate that you're missing History 236b; help you plan your future; and ponder the meaning of life with you.

But let me be honest with you. Your chances of getting a great advisor are about as good as of swatting a fly with a hammer. At nearly every college I've reviewed, advising is the #2 student complaint. (Parking is #1.) Why is advising usually so lousy? At most colleges, the quality of advising doesn't count when faculty are being considered for salary increases. So, if your advisor sounds like *he* needs advising, request a switch from the secretary of your major department.

> **Your chances of getting a great advisor are about as good as of swatting a fly with a hammer.**

The Virtual Advisor

No matter how good your advisor, chances are there is important stuff that your advisor doesn't know. So consult the advisor that's guaranteed to be knowledgeable: the college catalog, in print or at the college's Web site. It has most of what you need to know, is available 24 hours a day, seven days a week, and is guaranteed to cure your insomnia. Be sure to identify the courses you're required to take for graduation and for your major. That will help you get started early, and avoid ending up being a teary college senior who thinks she's going to graduate, only to find that she's missing some course that won't be offered for the next three semesters.

Finding a Mentor

A mentor is more than an advisor. He's a career and life coach. When you're applying to college, the idea of a mentor may sound good. Imagine a wise professor inviting you to coffee, you working at his or her elbow on an important research project, receiving door-opening letters of recommendation[13], and finding a lifetime friend.

---

[13] Half of students graduate from large colleges without knowing a single professor well enough to request a letter of recommendation.

But once at college, these visions are often replaced by new ones, such as appearing stupid in front of a professor. These visions cause students to avoid professors.

Fortunately, these visions are distorted. Professors don't expect undergraduates to be wise. Frankly, they expect them to be passive. So, if you take the initiative and ask questions (anything but "Will this be on the midterm?"), they'll respect you more. The vision of the inaccessible professor is sometimes incorrect. Even at large colleges, many professors are open to meeting with motivated students. And those meetings rarely are medieval torture treatments. A study found that the most frequently discussed topics are answering student questions about the course, job prospects, money, and careers, followed by boy/girlfriends, lifestyles, movies, popular music, world problems, and social events. Not quite the academic grilling you might have feared. If you're nervous about having to answer a question on the spot, try e-mail.

After a couple of meetings with a professor whom you like, take a risk. Ask, "Might you need a student assistant? Or could I do an independent study (see p. 122) with you?"

The thought of working for a professor may be intimidating. How can "average you" work for a brilliant professor? Relax. You don't need to be a genius. She's got the genius. What she needs is someone earnest, reliable, and enjoyable to work with. That would be you.

Many students feel more comfortable getting advice and personal attention from someone other than a professor. That's okay. See a resident assistant in your dorm, a friendly classmate, an older student, a teaching assistant, someone in your major department's student organization, a member of the student honor society, someone who works in the office of student affairs, a campus chaplain, or someone from the college's student learning center.

CRITICAL DECISION #16: WHAT CLASSES SHOULD I TAKE? HOW MANY?

Top Five Rules for Choosing Courses

1. Unless you're a strong student, for the first term, take four courses rather than the usual five. Just getting used to college life is a course in itself. Let one course be in your prospective major; take one or two that fulfill requirements for graduation; and pick another course simply because it sounds exciting.

2. Take mainly standard courses your first year, for example, Introduction to Biology, English Composition, Western Civilization. These courses usually meet graduation requirements no matter what your major, and if, by any chance, you decide to transfer, most colleges will award you credit for these courses.

3. Limit yourself to one or two killer courses per term. Most students find the following courses tough: chemistry, physics, calculus, literature (lots of reading).

    On most campuses, most students find these easier: introductory courses in psychology, education, sociology, women's studies, ethnic studies, physical education, music, and art.

4. Even large colleges offer some small classes. Try to take at least one per term, for example, a freshman seminar, a course in a living/learning program (see pp. 157–158), or an honors class. Often you can find one that will meet a graduation requirement. Small classes not only may teach you more, they're a source of friends—you're having discussions with a dozen students for 10 to 15 weeks, so there's bound to be someone you click with.

5. If your goal is to transfer, contact the college to which you want to transfer before registering for your first semester at your first college. Find out which courses the second college wants you to take. Get it in writing!

IMPORTANT RULE: When in doubt, choose the teacher rather than the course title. European Linguistics taught by a great teacher is usually better than Human Sexuality taught by a dud.

Ways to Find Life-transforming Professors

Ask at orientation.

Ask students.

Ask your advisor or other professor, especially one whose class you liked.

Consult the list of teaching award winners. It's usually in the catalog or at the office of academic affairs.

Check student ratings of professors. At the end of most college courses, students fill out a form evaluating their instructors. At some colleges, students have access to the results. Check with the student government office.

Attend a meeting of the club for students majoring in your field. Ask who's good.

Ask the department secretary, teaching assistants, resident assistants, and other students.

Ask the department secretary for a copy of the syllabus. This describes the course and lists the required readings and assigments.

Look at the required books in the bookstore.

Talk with the professor about his or her upcoming course.

I love this one: Overenroll. If you're planning on taking five courses, enroll for six. Go to the first class meeting of all six, then drop the worst. No need to put up with a professor who speaks incomprehensible English or one who assigns umpteen incomprehensible books.

Top Seven Rewarding Courses

1. **Courses in real-life survival skills.** Take a course in public speaking, a writing course, public relations, word processing/spreadsheets/databases, business, human sexuality, or the Internet.

   A special pitch for writing courses. They're usually taught in a small class in which you'll get valuable feedback on your writing. Write better and you'll do better in most of your other courses. Equally as important, writing improves your thinking skills, and believe me, you could use that—even if you got As in high school English. And if you're thinking, "Yuck, I hate writing," that's all the more reason to take it.

2. **Independent study** (also called a tutorial). An independent study is not tutoring. It's a one-on-one course with your choice of professor on a topic of your choice that isn't covered in a regular course. It sounds scary, but it's usually much more interesting and custom-tailored than a regular course. How do you get a tutorial? Just ask a cool professor. Surprisingly, even at large colleges, she often will say yes. If so, you and the prof will jointly decide what you'll read, and then meet every week or two to grill you to uncover your every weakness. (Just kidding.) You'll usually write a paper or two and then receive course credit. It's a way to study what you want, with whom you want, in a class of one! Great letters of recommendation often result. Taking a few independent studies is one of the smartest things you can do at college.

> **Taking a few independent studies is one of the smartest things you can do at college.**

3. **Honors classes.** Typically, these are small classes with top students taught by the best professors. That's what I call a patch of Ivy.

4. **Study abroad programs.** In looking back, many college graduates said they grew most from studying abroad.

INSIDER'S SECRET: Even if you don't plan on studying abroad until your junior year of college, start investigating now. Many top programs have very early deadlines.

5. **Courses with discussion sections.** In these, for two or three hours a week you sit listening to a lecture. Then for one hour a week, the large lecture is broken up into small discussion groups, usually led by a graduate student. This can be a nice blend; you get to hear the ideas of the brilliant professor yet enjoy the personal attention and more active learning that comes from a small class led by a graduate student.

6. **New ideas classes.** One of college's main purposes is to expose you to new ideas. If your politics are conservative, take a course on Marx. If you think government should aid the unfortunate, attend an objectivist or skeptics club meeting. You'll feel more secure in your viewpoint, be better able to defend your position to others or to yourself, or you might even change your views. College offers a unique opportunity to grow.

> One of college's main purposes is to expose you to new ideas. If your politics are conservative, take a course on Marx. If you think government should aid the unfortunate, attend an objectivist or skeptics club meeting.

7. **Cooperative Education:** No, this doesn't mean you do each other's term papers. Co-op education refers to internships that earn college credit. (See p. 163 for information.)

Crashing a Class

You try to register for a class. The perhaps digitized voice says, "I'm sorry. Course closed." The savvy student, if he really wants the class, ignores the voice, runs to the professor's office before the first day of class, and asks to be added to the class roll: "I really want to take your class because [*insert amazing reason here*]." If the professor says no, the student responds, "Well might I just sit in? If, by any chance, enough students drop the course, maybe you'll allow me to enroll. And if worse comes to worst, even if I can't enroll, I will have learned the material." You'll usually get in.

CRITICAL DECISION #17: HOW CAN I GET COURSE CREDIT THE EASY WAY?

Advanced Placement

If you've scored at least 3 on an Advanced Placement exam, be sure your college transcript shows that you've received credit for that course. Some colleges insist on a 4.

International Baccalaureate

Many colleges award credit for International Baccalaureate cours-es taken in high school. Check to be sure they've credited you.

CLEP

The same folks who bring you the SAT exams have another test. You may be happy to take this one. If you pass a 90-minute exam in any of dozens of subjects, most colleges will credit you with a full col-lege course! Before starting to study for these exams, check with your college to make sure they'll give you credit. If so, for exam informa-tion call: 609-771-7865 or visit *www.collegeboard.org*.

Challenge a Course

Think you know enough about a subject to pass the final exam even if you haven't taken the course? Perhaps by studying the text-book? Or because of your life experience? If so, ask the professor of the course if you can "chal-lenge" the course. Most profes-sors will agree to give you the equivalent of a final exam. Pass and you get credit for the entire course!

> **Are you a so-so student but would love to see what it's like to attend a designer-label college? Many—for example, Berkeley and Cornell—are nearly open admission during the summer.**

Summer School

Want a way to make a tough course easier? Take it during the summer. Classes are generally smaller, professors are in a better mood, and you only have that one monster course to concentrate on.

Are you a so-so student but would love to see what it's like to at-tend a designer-label college? Many—for example, Berkeley and Cornell—are nearly open admission during the summer. But check with your advisor to be sure the course credit will transfer.

Summer school has downsides. "Some dorms and classroom buildings aren't air-conditioned. They're ovens . . . Also, a stint of boring, fatiguing summer school may leave you in a foul mood as you begin the fall term."[14]

---

[14] Worthington and Farrar, *Ultimate College Survival Guide*

Correspondence Courses

Visit *www.petersons.com* or get a copy of the *Independent Study Catalog* (Peterson's, revised periodically). They list thousands of text-, audio-, or videotape-based courses that you can take in the comfort of your room, at your own pace, usually at a bargain price. Many colleges will accept these courses in place of their own, but check with your advisor to be sure. Beware: Only one-third of students who start a correspondence course ever finish it. They are terrific for the self-starter, a risk for the procrastinator.

CRITICAL DECISION #18: HOW AM I GOING TO LEARN SOMETHING IN THIS CLASS?

Most of us want to get good grades, acquire skills, and have time left for fun. That's what this section is all about—minimally painful ways to boost your grades and ensure you remember something of value long after the course is over.

Ways to Stay Awake and Learn Something

Read first. If you've done the assigned reading before rather than after class, you'll understand the lecture better, and so be more likely to stay awake. If it's a discussion class, you're more likely to participate, which also helps you stay awake. Most important: **show up.**

Martin Spethman, author of *How to Get into and Graduate from College in Four Years,* points out the problem. "You skip class because you are behind, don't want to be called on, or the lecturer is boring. So you'll have to rely on the notes of someone who was there, which means they probably won't be clear to you. So, by next class, you'll be further behind. You can break the vicious cycle: Go to just one lecture prepared, change your seat, and sit next to someone cute to keep you wanting to come." (Get your mind out of the gutter.)

Sit in a power seat. Everyone knows it's easier to pay attention in the front seats, but there's more to it than that. Each instructor's eyes tend to focus on one area, for example, one-quarter of the way back and slightly to one side of center. These power seats are the places to be. From there, the instructor is more likely to see your positive eye contact and frequently raised hand. Besides, it's hard to chat, doodle, or read the college newspaper with the teacher's eyes beaming at you every few seconds like searchlights. Power seats are the places to be, but I know some students who would rather sit anywhere than in a power seat, especially if it's a lousy prof. Ironically, that's when a power seat is most important.

Don't let a lousy prof mess you up. The kiss of death is to think; "I can't learn from this guy. I don't like him." Or "She has this terrible accent." Anyway, now you're stuck, so your reaction to a lousy teacher has to be, "I'll work twice as hard." It's easy to do well with a great teacher, but they're not that common because at most colleges, professors are hired and promoted more on how much research they do than on how well they teach. Good students learn how to avoid the worst professors and learn plenty from the average ones. Author Martin Spethman, in *How to Get Into and Graduate from College in Four Years,* advises, "Make them earn their money. Don't let them race through a lecture without explaining clearly anything you don't understand."

Get active. When you find yourself spacing out, listen hard for 10 to 20 seconds, then ask yourself; "What should I do? Take a note, say something, apply the professor's comment to my life, or do nothing?" Keep doing that and you'll stay awake, the time will go more quickly, and you'll learn more.

By the way, asking a question or making a comment is a triple winner. It makes you learn more, you get personalized feedback, and you impress the teacher. As a former prof, I know that instructors appreciate all questions. Even a dumb question lets us know the student cares and gives us feedback on what was and wasn't clear. What we hate is indifference—bored faces and slouching bodies. **Rule of thumb:** in discussion classes, speak up one to three times per hour.

What if you want to make a comment or ask a question in a class of 150 students? Write it in the margin and speak to the instructor after class, during the discussion section, or during the professor's office hours.

Take a Moderate Amount of Notes

The lecture. You're going to have to endure lots of these often boring one-way communications. Unfortunately, you'll also be tested on them. That means take good notes or die.

Ready for some good news? The best note takers write fairly little, jotting down only the phrases (never whole sentences) that summarize the main concepts and a few important specifics *that they do not know*. Even if it's important, don't write something you already know. Because you're not writing all the time, you have time to think about what the instructor is saying. You'll leave class having already understood much of the material and with a manageable amount of notes to review. Rmbr. Take a mod amt of notes. Ok?

The best note takers write fairly little, jotting down only the phrases (never whole sentences) that summarize the main concepts and a few important specifics *that they do not know.*

How do you know what you can skip? Write when the instructor seems to be emphasizing a point. How can you tell? Tip-offs include when he slows the rate of speech, repeats himself, writes on the board, uses hand gestures, speaks louder, spends a lot of time on one point, or uses phrases that let you know he's saying something important: "The main point is," "Therefore," "To summarize," "Let me make this clear," or the subtle, "On the test I might ask..."

If you wonder whether your notes are any good, show them to your prof. If she rolls on the floor laughing, listen up and try again.

Great idea from college counselor Mary Beth Kravats: If you're a bad note taker, record lectures using a small tape recorder that has a three-digit tape counter. Take notes as usual, but when you're stuck, write the tape counter number, so later you can find that part of the tape quickly.

Handouts from the professor are very likely to find their way onto tests. Attach them to your notes.

Don't cram. Good note takers lock in their learning by rereading and maybe even reorganizing their notes that day, to make sure they're in good enough shape to be useful in studying for the test. It can be helpful and fun to do it with a smart classmate. You may be able to fill in what the partner missed.

If you don't fix your notes right after class, your notes will probably miss one-quarter of what you need. That means you start with a C, even if you remember everything. If something in your notes is unclear, make a note to ask about it the next day. A day or two before the test, good note takers usually only need to do a brief general review and then focus on any weak spots. No cramming and probably a good test score.

At the end of the course, I know it's tempting to throw away your notes, but don't—they might help in another course, and at minimum, they'll have big-time nostalgia value. I guarantee that 20 years from now, you'll be amazed to see how much you've forgotten.

CRITICAL DECISION #19: PREPPING FOR TESTS

Ways to Get an A *and* Remember Something Afterwards (Even if You're Not a Genius)

Study after each class: Revise your notes and read the chapter. Cramming is the kiss of death. Even if, after cramming, you do well on the test (doubtful), you'll forget most of it two seconds after the test. So, you'll have wasted all that time and tuition just to have a good time. You can do that at home for free.

It's often tough to study in your dorm. Use these sources of peace and quiet: a quiet room in the residence hall or the library (not the room in which everyone's flirting); outdoors under a tree; chapel; tutoring center; park bench; in your car; an empty classroom; a coffeehouse with booths so you can stretch out.

Ever finish reading an assignment and wonder what it was about? Here's a surefire preventive. As you read, follow each line down with your hand. This helps you stay focused and keeps you from losing your place. **Read only a paragraph or two, then turn**

away and recite what you remember. If you've left out something important, say it aloud and, in the margin, bracket that part so you can reread it just before the test.

IMPORTANT: When reciting, pause a few seconds between sections; otherwise, you won't remember it. Try the above technique on the next paragraph.

Or even easier, when you feel yourself spacing out, read the important stuff aloud. It's hard to space out while reading aloud. Also you'll remember it better because you're going slowly and because you're hearing your voice at the same time as you're seeing the words.

If you don't understand a section, reread it only once. If you still don't understand it, just mark it with a question mark, and go on. Nothing is more frustrating than staying stuck. At the end of the chapter, call a friend or ask the instructor about your question marks. This approach to reading also works well when studying your class notes.

Write a response. After reading a section, write whatever you want about it. For example; what made you angry, happy, or confused about what you read? What do you most want to remember? Is any of it relevant to your life?

Pace the floor while studying hard stuff. Walking increases the circulation to the brain.

Use different highlighters for different stuff. Try hot pink for the stuff most likely to be on the exam and yellow for other stuff worth highlighting. Not only does this keep you awake, the color is a memory jogger.

Ask the instructor what to focus on in studying for a test. You'll likely get more help by asking during an office hour. "Any suggestions as to the wisest approach to studying for the exam?"

For memorization tests, make flash cards at least a week in advance. If you make them up last-minute, you'll spend most of your time making and little memorizing.

Every week, meet with one, two, or three study partners. Take turns asking your partners questions you think could be on the test. But one U.S.C. student warned, "Between the fool-around time and the time helping a girl who didn't prepare for the study group, I would have learned more if I studied by myself. I did have a good time, though." Moral of the story: Choose your study partners carefully.

Create a pretend crib sheet. Imagine that the instructor allowed you to bring one sheet of paper of notes into the exam. What would you write (small handwriting permitted)? On the night before the exam, just study that sheet.

Avoid guilt. A student once asked me, "I've heard that no matter how much you study, you can't read everything that's required. Is that true?" I met with the Student Honor Society at Berkeley, some of the best students at the nation's most prestigious public university. Every one of these superstudents agreed that it's impossible to read everything that is required, let alone recommended. Rest assured that no professor will assign the McVersion. Some profs give assignments as though their course is the only one you're taking. Here are a few ways to deal with the problem of too much to read.

> It's impossible to read everything that is required, let alone recommended.

Read what you like. Some students personalize their education by devoting most effort to what they're interested in. They do enough work on their other subjects to get acceptable grades, but save the extra effort for the courses they're most interested in.

Flexible reading. Read the way you drive a car. There are times to read at 60 mph, other times at 30, and when you get to hard but important concepts, it's stop-and-go.

Skim the book with *Cliff's Notes* or *Barron's Book Notes*. This may be the only option if the professor expects you to read *Ulysses* in one week. *Cliff's* or *Barron's Book Notes* provide a plot summary and analysis of themes, characters, and symbolism.

Top Six Keys to Successful Test Taking

6. Have you ever written four essays and found out later that the instructions said, "Choose three of four"? The easiest way to boost your test score is to read the directions and questions carefully. If you're not sure of what's being asked, don't be afraid to ask the instructor.

5. The most important test-taking skill? Knowing how to conquer the tough questions. Even A students encounter items they're unsure of, but instead of getting flustered and making a wild guess, they spend some extra seconds figuring out a way to make an intelligent one.

4. When I was in the seventh grade, our science teacher told us that on a multiple-choice test, when you're absolutely stuck between two choices, choose the one that's closest to the middle because test makers tend to hide the correct answer in the middle. I'm not sure he's right, but I always followed his advice whenever two choices looked equally good. It just felt better to have some way of choosing.

3. On essay tests, first read all the questions, then begin with the easiest one and work your way up. This way, if you don't have time to finish, the hardest essay will be left undone. Also, doing easier essays builds confidence and may even trigger thoughts on the hard ones.

2. You get the test back. Don't do what I did when I was in college, which was look at the grade, quickly scan the red marks, and stuff the test into my notebook. Look carefully at those red marks. They are individualized feedback, the stuff that private colleges charge big bucks for.

1. Think of the returned test paper as a study plan for the next exam. The College Board says, "Virtually all students study *for* tests. Good students study *from* tests," especially the wrong answers. Look at each error you made. What can you learn from that error, both for your learning and as a clue to how to do better on the next test? Then look at the test as a whole. Did the exam focus on big concepts or trivial facts? On material from class or from the text? The next test will likely be similar.

CRITICAL DECISION #20: I'VE GOT THIS PAPER TO WRITE

Most of you are lousy writers, even if you got As in high school English. There are so few good writers that many teachers give As to marginal performers. And, as I've stressed, writing is crucial. Write well and your overall G.P.A. will likely jump. More important, you'll always need to write, from work memos to love letters.

Ten Steps to a Better Paper

Step 1: Choose a topic that you care about, perhaps related to a career or personal interest.

Step 2: If at all possible, use a sub-notebook or notebook computer.

Step 3: If necessary, do some preliminary reading, for example, an overview article to help you develop a thesis or focus for your paper. (Your focus may change as you're doing Step 4.)

Step 4: If you need to do research, write your notes and ideas on a computer so it's easy to move things around. The Internet is an amazing tool. (Check out my favorite search engine, *www.metacrawler.com*, and my favorite gateway to periodical resources, *www.elibrary.com*.) If you don't have a computer, write one piece of information per index card.

Step 5: Place each piece of information into one of a few categories. This will be the structure of your paper.

Step 6: Within each category, put each piece of information in a logical order.

Step 7: Turn these ordered pieces of information into smooth paragraphs. Add and subtract material as you see fit.

Don't spend much time just staring at the screen. Keep adding, subtracting, and revising stuff even if you're not sure the changes are good. The constant changing keeps you feeling like you're making progress, and probably sooner rather than later, your product will get better and better.

Step 8: Write an introduction and conclusion. Don't stare at a blank screen. Write whatever comes to mind and revise. It's much easier to revise than to generate brilliance out of thin air.

Step 9: Put your paper away for a day and then revise again.

Step 10: Show a draft to the person who will be grading the paper: the professor or teaching assistant. Often, he'll be willing to read a draft. That almost ensures a good grade when you submit your final version. If he refuses, try one of the campus' writing tutors, a friend, or even your parent. If you get a bad grade, ask the instructor if you can rewrite based on his feedback and resubmit. If he says yes, it's an almost guaranteed way to improve your grade.

> **Don't stare at a blank screen. Write whatever comes to mind and revise. It's much easier to revise than to generate brilliance out of thin air.**

Help!

Worthington and Farrar warn that you will run into problems at college. It's inevitable. But they also point out the good news, that "college is one of the few situations in life in which hundreds of people exist simply to help you find your way. Counselors, tutors, faculty and resident assistants, financial aid people, health care workers, librarians, campus security, members of the clergy—they're all there for you. If you're hesitant to use their services, remember that your tuition helps pay for their presence. Not using these services is like driving up to the gas pump, paying for $10 worth and driving off after getting just $5 worth."[15] Also remember that it's no shame to use these services. Even many top students use them.

The most important thing is to do something *now*. Don't hold off until finals when it's too late. Take an honest look at yourself and figure out why you're doing badly. If it's an emotional problem, see a campus counselor. If you're not understanding the material, get a

---

[15] Worthington and Farrar, *Ultimate College Survival Guide.*

tutor. If your professor hates your papers, see him or her. If you're not spending enough time studying, reserve more study time each week, as rigidly scheduled as if it were an additional class. If a class is miles over your head, consider dropping it.

CRITICAL DECISION #21: "I JUST DON'T GET IT."

O'Neil Turner quotes Tom Hanks, the manager in A League of Their Own. *Hanks tells a player, "Of course it's hard. It's supposed to be hard. If it wasn't hard, everyone would do it. It's the hard that makes it great."*

Whether it's reading, writing, math, time management, study skills, or test anxiety, academic problems are more common than rice in China. Fortunately, there's help available on any campus. Don't let pride keep you from getting extra help if you need it.

Six Lines of Defense Against an Academic Problem

1. If you found a class session difficult (and that can be the very first session), **be sure you did the basics:** Did you read the material before class, concentrate hard in class, and review your class notes immediately after class? If not, try those things before doing anything else. If that doesn't work, proceed to step 2.

2. Before the next class, **see the professor or teaching assistant.** They're usually impressed that you cared enough to seek help. Come in with specific questions you want help with. "I didn't understand the lecture" is not specific.

3. **A one-on-one tutor is the most potent way to improve.** And often the best and least expensive tutor is a student in your class. She's been attending your class sessions, reading your course readings, and solidifies her own knowledge by teaching it to you. Student tutors are a bargain—you may only need to pay $6 to $10 an hour, perhaps for only a few hours. Just go up to a student who appears to know the material and seems like a patient person. Explain that you need a tutor. If you can't find someone in your class, ask your professor or the department secretary for a recommendation.

4. **Go to the campus' tutoring center.**

5. **If it's going to require too much effort to survive a class, drop it,** but be sure you use the extra time on the remaining classes, not hanging out with your sweetie.

6. **If necessary, switch to an easier major**—even if your parents would love you to be a doctor. Tell them that if you don't switch, you're going to need a doctor.

CRITICAL DECISION #22: "I'M UNHAPPY."

Top Ten Ways to Get Happier

10. Ask yourself, **"What has worked in the past to solve the problem?** Can I use that solution now?"

9. Ask yourself, **"What would my best self do to solve my problem?"** "What would my role model do?"

8. Talk into a mirror. **Pretend you were giving advice to your twin** who was feeling exactly as you are.

7. **Take your mind off your worries by immersing yourself in something constructive.** Get to work or help someone else. If you get a bad test score, go and study for an hour. If you just had a fight with a friend, go jogging.

   A variant on that is to choose a very ambitious goal, for example, deciding that you're going to be the next editor-in-chief of the student newspaper. Soon you might find yourself saying, "I don't have time to feel sorry for myself."

   I know a psychologist who is bedridden for life with multiple sclerosis. He spoke of committing suicide because he felt useless. I suggested that as a psychologist with multiple sclerosis, there are few people on earth more qualified to provide support and friendship by phone to other bedridden people, especially those with MS. He started calling members of the local MS society and not only helped them, but having found some purpose, no longer talks of suicide. He talks of charging for his counseling services.

> **The more you do, the more you'll feel you can do. The less you do, the less you'll feel you can do.**

The more you do, the more you'll feel you can do. The less you do, the less you'll feel you can do.

6. **If you need self-pity time, give yourself a finite amount.** Say, for example, "At 4:00, I'm going to start to solve this problem by making an appointment with a tutor."

5. **Fake it 'til you make it.** If you're feeling anxious, be an actor and pretend you're carefree. It's amazing, but after a while, you may forget that you were pretending.

4. **Talk with your parents or a wise friend.**

3. **Start a peer support group.** Ask a few friends if they'd like to get together for a Thank God It's Friday session. If the first session goes well, schedule another.

2. **See an on-campus counselor.** Many students think that counseling is only for the screwed up. Not true. At some time, all of us have felt depressed, lonely, inadequate, unmotivated, indecisive, socially inept, test phobic, self-destructive, or aimless. Most colleges offer free group and individual counseling, and workshops on these as well as concerns such as time management, drugs/alcohol, eating disorders, insomnia, sexuality, choosing a major or career, and stress reduction.

> **An emotional problem that has lasted for years is often a physical problem that can be helped with medication. See a doctor.**

An emotional problem that has lasted for years is often a physical problem that can be helped with medication. See a doctor.

Some students worry that if they see a campus counselor, their parents might find out their deep dark secrets. Don't worry. Under almost all circumstances, the college cannot legally release information to your parents without your permission. Worthington and Farrar reassure, "You're very unlikely to have your parent ask you, 'Andre, I'm a little confused. This report from the student health service says you were treated for syphilis. How can that be?' "

1. **Do something about your problem. If it doesn't work, try something else.** The key to getting unstuck is trying things. Even if an approach doesn't work, you're better off than you are now. Each time you try an unsuccessful approach, you're a step closer to finding a successful one. So try something, even a simple thing like buying yourself a present to cheer you up. Trying nothing is the one approach that practically ensures you'll stay stuck.

Eating Disorders

This problem deserves its own category because anorexia (starving yourself) and bulimia (overeating and vomiting) has reached epidemic proportions among females and because it can kill. So, if you're eating less than 1,000 calories a day or are binging and purging, please get help. You might start with the free booklet, *Eating Disorders.* Get it by writing to the Consumer Information Catalog, P.O. Box 100, Pueblo, CO 81002 or download it from *www.pueblo.gsa.gov.* Want to read more? Contact the American Anorexia/Bulimia Association at 165 West 46th Street #1108, New York, NY 10036, 212-575-6200, *members.aol.com/amanbu* Chances are, though, reading won't be enough. If not, start at your college's counseling or health center. If they don't have an eating disorders specialist on staff, they should be able to refer you to one off campus—you are far from the first person to ask for help. For an ongoing discussion on eating disorders, try the newsgroup *alt.support.eatingdisord*

CRITICAL DECISION #23: HOW ETHICAL DO YOU WANT TO BE?

I can't write a book for college-bound students without saying something about ethics. It worries me. Studies report that 75 percent of college students cheat on tests and papers. Throughout society, dishonesty seems the norm. Even the president of the United States, his wife, half his cabinet, the vice president, the speaker of the house, the head of the nation's largest black church, and hundreds of savings & loans have been recently investigated. A society in which people cannot trust each other is doomed.

But here, I'm not going to appeal to lofty ideals. Those of you with lofty ideals aren't going to cheat anyway. So I'll simply appeal to your self-interest. You may or may not get ahead by cheating. Some do, others don't. If you do cheat, as you get older you will cheat more not less, because you'll grow more dependent on it. It will lower your self-esteem. You may feel

> **If you do cheat, as you get older you will cheat more not less, because you'll grow more dependent on it.**

that if it weren't for cheating, you wouldn't have got as far as you have. You may feel like an imposter. And you'll have learned less, so you will likely fail more in life because there are many times you simply can't cheat—for example, in a presentation at a business meeting. And finally, when you're old and looking back on your life, you may not feel good about the person you were. There are few sadder feelings than feeling bad about how you lived your life. In the long run, the better grades you'll get from cheating will simply not compensate. Besides, you may get caught and kicked out of college.

So consider getting into the habit of being honest. When you walk into an exam, find a seat far away from anyone. Eliminate the possibility of cheating and you'll derive a side benefit—it will be easier to concentrate.

Every time you're writing a paper, remind yourself that your grade won't go down if you give credit to the author of a quote. It's so easy. If you want to use someone's ideas, fine. Just write, "As Joe Shmo said..." I have quoted many people in this book. Do you think less of me?

If you're thinking about letting someone else write a paper for you, remember that if they're writing it, they'll become a better writer/thinker and you won't. In the long run, you'll be the loser.

THE PERFECT PARENT: One reason that students cheat is to meet parental expectations. Make it perfectly clear that you'd rather see an honest C than a cheating A. And if you're not sure that's right, please read the previous section.

CRITICAL DECISION #24: AM I GOING TO TAKE WHATEVER COMES OR AM I GOING TO MAKE SURE I GET A FAIR DEAL?

If something is wrong with your college life, you or someone on campus can probably fix it.

Don't just accept a miserable roommate, weekends with nothing to do, a noisy room, a bad schedule, or a professor you can't understand. A freshman at the University of Alabama scored 1300 on the SAT but wasn't smart enough to ask for a roommate when

> **Think of this every time a problem arises: "Fix it. If you can't, ask. If someone says no, ask someone else."**

she was given a single room. She suffered in loneliness for an entire semester, when undoubtedly there were hundreds of women who would have loved to trade for her single.

A member of the orientation committee at Harvard gives the following advice to incoming students. If you think of this every time a problem arises, you'll be on the path to college heaven. She advises, "Fix it. If you can't, ask. If someone says no, ask someone else."

CRITICAL DECISION #25: SHOULD I TRANSFER?

At some point, many college students wonder if they should transfer to another college. Often their problems would transfer along with them, for example, under-preparedness for college-level work or poor social skills. These students should look inward for solutions.

Other students think about transferring the first time they cry.

Give it at least a full semester before seriously considering a change. Might any of these help? Try a new roommate, a lighter or heavier courseload, more carefully picking professors, participating in an extracurricular activity, reaching out to make friends. Certainly, before tackling the huge hassle of transferring, talk with everyone you trust—wise friends, parents, siblings, your resident assistant, advisor, or even a head honcho at the college.

One more way to avoid the pain of transferring is to try a semester at a campus with which your college offers exchange privileges. (See your college's catalog.)

Of course, there are good reasons to consider a transfer. O'Neil Turner suggests seven: (1) location, (2) size, (3) most classes are much too easy or too difficult, (4) money, (5) major, (6) social life misfit (for example, unalterably too dead or too wild), or (7) an incompatible coach.

If you think you might want to transfer, be sure you're taking courses that your new college will accept. The safest choices are standard introductory college-level courses, for example, introduction to chemistry, psychology, political science, sociology, American literature, European history, calculus, and a foreign language.

Apply to a number of colleges. One may give you credit for all the courses you've taken, while another may not count half of them. To maximize your chances, submit catalog copy and even syllabi for courses you've taken. If you need housing, be sure the colleges you're considering offer housing to transfer students.

It may be difficult to keep your grades up if you're unhappy at a college, but with low grades, fewer colleges will be willing to take a chance on you.

CRITICAL DECISION #26: WILL YOU GO AFTER YOUR DREAM CAREER?

If you haven't already figured out your dream career, do it. (See p. 195.) Use your college's career center to help you to polish your résumé and interviewing skills. But don't just passively look through the want ads and placement office listings and send out résumés. Fewer than 25 percent of jobs are obtained this way.

Talk with lots of people with the potential to hire you. Of course, family and friends are ideal targets, but also ask for names of alumni at your college's career center. If they say that your dream job doesn't exist, explain why it should. Or ask a potential employer about the goals and problems within the organization. Could those goals or problems be addressed by someone doing a version of your dream job?

The McVersion of Chapter 5: The Keys to a Great College Experience

Carefully choose where you're going to live. All dorms are not alike. The dorms that may sound boring (for example, the honors or technology dorm) are often the best. (Why? See p. 83.)

✓ Set ground rules with your roommate (see p. 98) and keep them.

✓ Know how to manage your time and conquer procrastination. Although you'll probably hate this, the key to getting a lot done may be to get to bed early and get up early. The second key is having (and using) a daily to-do list.

✓ The most potent method of overcoming procrastination is—no matter how yucky it feels—to force yourself to sit down and get started. Once you've started, you'll probably continue. FACT: The more you do, the more you'll want to do. The less you do, the less you'll want to do. If you get stuck, don't reread it ten times. Just go over it once more. If you still don't get it, mark it with a question mark and go on. Later, ask a friend or the professor about your question marks.

✓ Growth takes place one-on-one. The key to a good college experience is relationships with your roommate, friends, advisor, professor. If you're not happy with the ones you have, get new ones. Make a point of finding one or more wonderful professors who are willing to be your mentors.

✓ If you choose to drink alcohol, limit yourself to one or two drinks in an evening. If you drink more than that on a regular basis, you are in danger of becoming a permanent loser. Get help or get ready to throw your life away.

✓ Take classes from the best professors. How to find them? Ask other students or the department secretary, consult the list of teaching award winners that is available from the office of academic affairs, and the student ratings of professors (if available). Overenroll—if you want five courses, sign up for six. Attend the first class of all six and drop the worst one.

✓ Learn survival skills; become a good writer and public speaker. Learn how to use the Internet efficiently.

✓ Show up for class and sit in a power seat, the seats where the professor focuses his eyes most of the time. As Woody Allen says, "80 percent of success is showing up."

✓ Be an active learner. Students who make comments and ask questions learn more. Even if your question is dumb, the professor and non-jerk students will appreciate your asking. It may be the question they were too self-conscious to ask.

✓ Get a sub-notebook computer—great for taking notes in class, doing research in the library, and writing your paper under a tree. Make sure it doesn't get ripped off.

✓ Study on your own, but once a week (or certainly before an exam), meet with one or two study partners in each class. Take turns asking each other questions that you think might be on the test. Then try to come up with good answers.

✓ Don't cheat. Even if you don't get caught, after you graduate you'll feel like an imposter. And cutting corners becomes more and more of a habit, which increases your chances of getting caught or feeling like an imposter. As a cheater, you'll know less. Like your sixth grade teacher always said, "You're only hurting yourself."

✓ When there's a problem, don't let it slide. It will only get worse. Try to fix it. If you can't, ask someone. If they can't help, ask someone else. Not using campus support services when you need them is like driving into a gas station, paying $10 and driving off with only $5 worth of gas.

✓ If you're struggling in class, consider hiring a classmate as a tutor.

✓ If you're depressed or anxious, do something about it. Start by trying to fix it yourself. Ask yourself, "What has helped me with this in the past?" If that doesn't work, speak with a wise friend or family member. If that doesn't work, see an on-campus counselor or a physician. Depression and anxiety can often be helped with medication and/or talk therapy.

✓ Don't be afraid to fail. If you always hit the target, you're probably standing too close. When I was at Berkeley, I wasted a great opportunity. I had small classes taught by smart professors who were more than willing to give me as much time as I needed. But I was so afraid of appearing dumb that I never asked a question that might possibly reveal my ignorance, and I never took on a really challenging project. Yes, I got my degree, but I got only half as much out of it as I could have.

APPENDICES

APPENDIX A

Want Help Figuring Out What You Want in a College?

DECISION 1: Do I want to consider two-year colleges? Four-year colleges? Both? This can help you decide:

Top Ten Reasons to Consider Starting at a Two-year College (even if you're a good student)

Put a checkmark next to each reason that is important to you. See if your parents mark what you mark.

10. Good teachers.

SURPRISE: Teachers are often better at two-year colleges. Why? Because they're hired and promoted on how well they teach, not on how much research they crank out.

9. On average, classes are smaller.

8. You'll probably learn as much. Probably because of #10 and #9 above, research indicates that students at two-year colleges learn as much as they would have in two years at a four-year college.

7. It's often easy to transfer from a two-year to a good four-year college.

Good grades at a two-year college and recommendations from your instructors can help wipe out a bad high school record. After two years of saving money and getting what can be a better-than-brand-name education, you may be able to transfer to a harder-to-get-into four-year college that would not have admitted you as a freshman. Bonus: your bachelor's diploma from a four-year brand-name college will look the same as if you had started there as a freshman.

6. It's a bargain.

Not only will most two-year colleges save your parents big bucks, you're more likely to graduate without loans to pay back, and you can save up for a cool place to live, that set of wheels, or more school.

5. You'd do better with less pressure.

Even some good students do better starting out in the more relaxed academic environment of a two-year college. At many two-year colleges, there are classes that attract top students—honors classes or courses like physics, philosophy, calculus, and poetry. Myth: Two-year colleges are only for dummies. There are some fine students at two-year colleges and some pretty dim bulbs at four-year institutions.

4. It's a place where weak students are more likely to succeed.

College work is usually harder than high school. If your high school grade point average in academic subjects is less than 2.7 (below B– or 80) and your SAT I score is below 900 (ACT below 19), your chances of succeeding at a four-year college are poor. Fewer than 20 percent of such students graduate even when given five years. In other words, if five such students start college, only one will get a diploma. And importantly, even if you squeak by, you may well end up competing for jobs requiring college-level academic skills, which are not your strength. Two-year colleges offer lots of classes and out-of-class support designed for students who are weak in reading, writing, or math.

And know this. Two-year colleges offer courses to prepare you for many good careers that don't require a four-year degree, for example, telecommunications engineering technology, food preparation (chef), robotics, aircraft repair, and respiratory therapy (the people who take care of the many cigarette smokers still out there).

3. There are many housing choices. Some students are better off with another year or two at home. Besides, the *Animal House*-type fun in a dorm is only fun for so long—it's frustrating trying to crank out that paper while your hallmates are cranking tunes. And how do you feel about sharing a bathroom with two dozen people—including members of the opposite sex?

If you do want to live in a dorm, a small percentage of two-year colleges do have dorms. If you decide to live in an apartment, you usually get your own room instead of being stuffed two or even three to a closet-sized dorm. And you get to choose your roommate.

2. **You can usually go part time or at night, as well as during the day,** so it's easy to have a job while at a two-year college.

1. **They're easy to get into.**

   As good as two-year colleges are, you'd think they'd be tough to get into, but most are 98.6 schools—virtually all you need to get in is normal body temperature. Most two-year colleges are open to all high school graduates, and the application usually doesn't require the SAT I, ACT, nor an essay.

Top Six Reasons to Consider Starting at a Four-year College

6. **You want mainly A and B students in your classes.**

   You're the sort of student who will learn more if your classmates are good students. You suspect that at a two-year college, the many low achievers might tempt you to goof off. Many four-year colleges also have lots of weak students, but the small percentage of colleges that are filled with top students are almost all four-year colleges.

5. **You want a college with a rich intellectual and cultural life.**

   Four-year colleges are more likely to have a large library, many guest speakers, clubs, well-attended football and basketball games, political demonstrations, and big-name concerts. Of course, not all four-year colleges are like this.

4. **You want a strong sense of campus community.** At four-year colleges, many students are involved in on-campus sports, clubs, the student newspaper, orchestra, and so on. In contrast, many two-year colleges (although not most private two-year colleges) are "grab and go" schools—many students just grab their classes and go home.

3. **You want to attend a college at which many students live on campus.** Four-year colleges are more likely to offer on-campus housing. Living on campus makes it easier to get to know other students and to have those late-night discussions about the meaning of life and the meaning of the home team's win.

2. **You deeply want to attend a brand-name college.** Even though you know you could start out at a two-year college and then finish up at a more prestigious four-year college, you'd feel very sad that you were starting off at a two-year college.

1. **It's easier to stay focused on schoolwork** at a four-year college. At most two-year colleges, you can go to class at night or part time, which enables you to take a job, even full time. So many two-year college students are tempted to put most of their energy into their job.

Now, in light of what you've read, what's best for you? Circle "two-year," "four-year," or both on your *What I Want* list on p. 2. Before deciding, you might discuss it with your parent or a counselor.

Here comes a very important but confusing part. Stay with me. I'll try to make it as simple as I can.

DECISION 2: Do I want a college with:

✓ mainly A students (with 1250–1600 SAT I or 28–36 ACT)

✓ mainly B to A students (with 1050–1250 SAT I or 22–27 ACT)

✓ an honors program and mainly B students

✓ mainly B– to C students (with 900–1100 SAT I or 18–21 ACT)

If you're a B to A student, you may be happiest at a college with mainly B to A students. But maybe not. (See, I told you it gets confusing.)

Top Five Reasons to Drop Down One Category

Put a checkmark next to any of these reasons that are important to you. See if your parents mark what you marked.

5. **You'll be one of the better students at that college.**
That usually means more personal attention from the professors. Imagine how you'd feel if a professor called you over after class, complimented you on your good work, and invited you to help on a research project. Picture what it would be like to have professors eager to help you get a good job or get into top graduate schools. (Yes, top students from easy-to-get-into colleges do get into top graduate schools.)

4. **You're less likely to burn out.** The second most common complaint at the Student Health Service at Harvard is stress and burnout. At a less competitive college, you're less likely to burn out. Just as important, you'll have more time to get involved in out-of-class activities. Most college graduates feel that they learned more outside the classroom than in. Sandra, an A student in high school, attended a college with many B students. She had the time to be a peer health counselor on campus, student member of the faculty senate, a volunteer with pregnant teens in East L.A., managing editor of the feminist newspaper, member of an intramural crew team, and student and later teacher of a women's self-defense class. By the way, she graduated with a 3.9 G.P.A.

3. Because you're not routinely being stretched to the max, **you can risk trying a challenging course:** organic chemistry, anyone? You might even have time for a rollerblading trip into the next county.

2. **You'll probably graduate with better self-esteem.** It feels great to be a star student. You'll tend to forget that your peers weren't all Einsteins.

1. **Many of my happiest clients (and my daughter) attended a one-category-down college.**

Top Six Reasons to Jump Up One Category

6. **Classes tend to be more challenging, so if you can keep up you'll learn more.** Are you the sort who would feel, "Hey, I'm in the big time. Sure it's hard but it's worth working hard to keep up."?

5. **Outside-of-class discussions tend to be more stimulating**—a few more ideas, a little less gossip. Again, you'll learn more. Are you the sort who would feel good listening to all those smart people even if your comments aren't always the best?

4. **The atmosphere in the on-campus housing may be more interesting** and less centered on getting drunk, listening to loud music, and watching soap operas. Most students won't plan their schedules around *South Park*. Are you the sort who would appreciate arguing with friends until 2 A.M. about affirmative action, the benefits of development versus environmental protection, or the smartest way to land a cool career?

3. **Extracurricular activities such as the student newspaper and drama productions are generally of higher quality.** That can make you happier at college. One tiny example: it's nice, every day, to have the option of reading a student-written newspaper filled with thoughtful discussions about everything from sex to George W. Bush, from Pearl Jam to what's right and wrong with the college.

2. **You're a late bloomer, and know you'll do better in college than your high school grades and test scores suggest.**

1. **Employers and graduate schools will be more impressed.**

   This advantage may not be as big as it seems. Will you get lower grades at a college with better students? Would you get worse recommendations from professors than if you were the big fish in the less selective pond? If so, the career advantage of a harder-to-get-into college may vanish. Imagine that you were a boss and had two job candidates, one with A grades and great letters of recommendation from a moderately selective college and another with B grades and lukewarm recommendations from a highly selective college. Are you sure who you'd choose?

One Reason *Not* to Jump Up a Category

Bill Mayher, author of *The College Mystique*, warns, "Research shows that some of the least successful college students have been the ones who barely squeaked into the college of their choice and then spent far too much of their academic careers wondering if they had the right stuff to be there." James Wickenden, former director of Harvard's Office for Graduate and Career Plans, says of the premed students he worked with who didn't get into medical school, "Had those students gone to other, less competitive colleges…they might have realized their career goals."[1]

An Interesting Alternative for Top Students: An Honors Program at a College with Mainly B Students

In an honors program, you typically get to take one course each term in a small class with top students taught by one of the col-

---

[1] Patrick, M. "N is for Saying No to the Ivy League," *Journal of College Admission*, Summer, 1998, p. 3-5.

lege's best professors; in other words, a patch of Ivy at a regular ol' college. Many honors programs extend the Ivy experience outside the classroom by offering an honors dorm and special extracurricular activities, for example, getting to have a small group discussion with Spike Lee when he comes to give a lecture on campus. But most of your classes and extracurricular life can be with "regular" students. That can be a nice balance. The honors designation on the diploma can open doors to top careers or graduate school. Two financial bonuses: Some of the best honors programs are at public universities, which are less expensive than private colleges. Also, honors students often get tuition discounts.

Institutions known for their high-quality honors programs include: the Universities of Delaware, Georgia, Indiana, Maryland, Michigan, North Carolina, Ohio State, Oregon, Penn State, South Carolina, Texas, Utah, Virginia, Washington, and the College of William & Mary. (To quickly assess the quality of any college's honors program, see p. 15.)

If you want to shoot for a college that is one category higher

Can you be admitted to a college that is one category higher? It's easiest if:

✓ you're good enough to play for the varsity;

✓ you're Black, Hispanic, or Native American;

✓ your parent has donated big bucks to the college, especially if the library is named after him or her.

Your application will also get a boost if you're:

✓ from a small town far away from the college (colleges like students with unusual perspectives).

✓ applying to a college at which less than 45 percent of the students are of your gender. For example, women get an advantage at engineering colleges; men get a boost at former women's colleges such as Vassar, Mary Washington, Goucher, and Sarah Lawrence.

✓ a fine musician, actor, or artist. (No, an extraordinary talent for doing chalk drawings with your toes doesn't count.)

✓ a student leader at a regional or national level.

Even if you're none of the above, a strong application can sometimes do the trick. (Chapter 3, which begins on p. 41, shows you how to create one.)

Now, in light of what you've read, what's best for you? Circle "Mainly A," "Mainly B to A," or "Honors program at a college with mainly B students," or "Mainly B– to C+," on your *What I Want* list on p. 2. Before deciding, you might discuss it with your parent or counselor.

DECISION 3: How much am I willing to pay for college?

Most colleges won't put it to you this bluntly, but it's the truth. If your family's income is $50,000 to $120,000, over your four college years, you and your parents will probably have to cough up $50,000 to $120,000 *in cash* [2] (depending on the college's sticker price). In addition, you will need to take on $15,000 to $30,000 in loans, plus you may have to hold a part-time job during each of your college years. Remember—and this is very important to most families—if you take more than four years to graduate (and many students do!), you may get little or no financial aid for year five. Prospects are even worse for year six and beyond.

There is little evidence that a more expensive education results in more learning or better job prospects, so if your family earns $50,000 or more, you might first consider low- or mid-priced colleges even if you want a small college. There are some good small public colleges, two-year and four-year.

It can be especially tempting to consider designer-label private colleges like Yale or Stanford. But the cost/benefit of attending even

---

[2] You may get additional financial aid if you're
  a. an A student applying to a college with mainly B students.
  b. a star athlete.
  c. African American, Hispanic, or Native American, especially if your high school record is at least average for that college.

these schools is unclear. For example, almost 40 percent of 4,000 students surveyed at the nation's most prestigious colleges felt their college wasn't a good value.[3] To be fair, some experts believe they are worth the money, but your college coach is convinced that these experts are wrong unless your family can easily afford the sticker price or you get at least $10,000 per year in cash financial aid. See p. xii for my reasoning.

Definitely think twice before shelling out big bucks for large private colleges. They may be worth the money if you're offered a big cash discount, but if not, you may be able to find a similar education at a public university for (over four years) $40,000 to $90,000 less.

Now, in light of what you've read, what's best for you? Turn to your *What I Want* list and write the maximum per-year sticker price you're willing to consider. Most colleges' total cost is $11,000 to $18,000 per year ($48,000 to $80,000 for four years, assuming 3 percent annual increases) for the in-state public colleges, and $22,000 to $35,000 for private colleges ($92,000 to $150,000 for four years, assuming 3 percent annual increases). Before deciding, you might discuss it with your parent or counselor.

DECISION 4: What size college do I want?

Top 13 Reasons to Prefer Small Colleges (under 5,000 undergrads)

Put a checkmark next to any reasons that are important to you.

13. Small colleges often pay more attention to students' application essays, extracurriculars, and letters of recommendation. This may be important if your grades and test scores aren't so hot.

12. Small colleges may feel less intimidating. Within a few days, you will know where most things are on campus.

11. Small colleges are better for students who might not have the self-discipline needed to thrive amid the anonymity of a large college.

---

[3]Greene, Howard. *The Select: Realities of Life and Learning in America's Elite Colleges.* HarperCollins, 1998.

10. **You'll know most students.** Some students like the idea that when they walk across campus, they'll run into lots of people they know, which is fine unless you're having a bad hair day.

9. **Typical class size will be 20 to 25 rather than 100+.** This makes some students more likely to go to class, pay attention, participate, and do the work.

8. **Classes are taught mainly by professors,** and rarely by less qualified, less well-trained graduate students.

7. **Much class time is spent listening to what your classmates have to say.** However, some college students end up considering this a disadvantage.

6. **Students, on average, are more serious about learning.**

5. **You'll do more writing assignments and take fewer multiple-choice tests.** Sure, multiple-choice is easier, but writing is a really important skill. In addition, writing assignments teach you to think logically while multiple-choice tests usually mean

   a) regurgitate and forget.

   b) memorize rather than understand.

   c) all of the above.

4. **You'll get more feedback on your writing.** Don't you hate it when you do all that work and the teacher simply writes "B. Good job."? Of course, that's better than "D. What happened?"

3. **Professors are more accessible,** which means it's easier to find a mentor, have opportunities to work on a professor's research, and get meaningful letters of recommendation. At a large college, you'll have to stalk professors and impress them with your knowledge or, at least, your eagerness to learn.

2. **It's easier to get to play on varsity sports teams, host an on-campus radio show, and so on.**

1. **A higher percentage of students graduate within four years,** on average, compared with large colleges.

Top Eight Reasons to Prefer Large Colleges (over 5,000 undergrads)

8. **A large number of specialized courses and majors.** For example, almost all colleges offer a biology major, but a large college might also offer genetics, biophysics, and molecular biology. And within your major, you'll have more flexibility.

7. Large colleges offer **more teachers to choose from.** But you'll have to make an effort to find out who's good. (See p. 121.)

6. There's **an endless number of students to meet,** often from diverse backgrounds.

5. There are **hundreds of clubs and activities.**

4. On average, **professors are doing more important** research than at small colleges. Graduate students usually get first crack at being research assistants, but if you're a good student and get to know a professor, you may get a chance.

3. **You can be a social butterfly or a hermit.** At a small college, you usually develop a hard-to-change reputation in the first month. "Oh, Sally. She cheats."

2. Most weekends, you'll have an ample **choice of concerts, movies, lectures, and sports events,** which means you're not likely to get bored.

1. **You may enjoy feeling like part of something big and well known.** It somehow feels better to be able to say, "Hi, I go to U.C.L.A." rather than "Hi, I go to the University of Minnesota at Morris," even though Morris is a fine school.

Living-Learning Program: An option offering some benefits of both large and small colleges

In a living/learning program, a group of 50 to 300 academically motivated students at a large college live in one dorm. Each term, they take one class right in the dorm, usually a small class taught by a top professor who may also live in the dorm. (No, she won't be your roommate.) Also, there are usually special activities. For example, last time I visited Truman State University, on Sunday mornings at its Ryle College, coffee, bagels, and *The New York Times* were available in a central living room in the dorm. Students could hang out (some come in pajamas) and discuss anything they found interesting in the *Times*. Students in living-learning programs develop especially close bonds with each other because they, a small group, are living, learning, and often sharing meals together. (Food fights breed closeness.) Yet they participate fully in the main college—taking classes there and getting involved in extracurriculars. In short, living/learning programs offer some of the best of big and small schools, often at a public college price.

Some colleges with well-regarded living-learning programs: Michigan State University, Indiana University, University of Colorado at Boulder, the University of Illinois at Urbana-Champaign, San Diego State University, and the University of Michigan at Ann Arbor. Alas, most colleges don't have them.

Now, in light of what you've read, what's best for you? Circle "Small," "Large," or "Living/Learning Program" on your *What I Want* list on p. 2. Before deciding, you might discuss it with your parent or counselor.

DECISION 5: Do I want a college in the sticks or near a large city?

Most students are happier at a college near big-city attractions, such as pro sports, Phish in concert, internships at 15 corporations and 26 government agencies, seven Thai restaurants. Also, you don't have to drive three hours to get to a putt-putt airplane that takes you to a connecting flight that takes you to your flight back home.

But some students are happier at a rural college. You can breathe the air, walk without a body alarm, hike nearby, and enjoy a more relaxed pace of life. Most students find that they can survive without a shopping mall, pro sports teams, and multiplexes. And because there's less to do off campus, rural campuses offer a stronger sense of community. But beware: A frequent complaint at rural colleges is "There's nothing to do but drink." After a year or two at rural colleges, some students crave something new. Sometimes, a semester in a domestic or overseas exchange program can restore your sanity.

Now, in light of what you've read, what's best for you? Circle "In/near big city," or "Away from big city" on your *What I Want* list on p. 3. Before deciding, you might discuss it with your parent or counselor.

DECISION 6: Do I want a college near home?

Eighty-five percent of students attend college within a day's drive from home. One reason is the lower transportation costs. But the main reason is that going to college feels less scary to both parent and student if they know that coming home for the weekend is an option.

Why go far away? Because it's fun to experience something different. A California surfer will find New York City an eye-opener—not just the winters, the people. Another plus for faraway colleges is that while a great-fit college might not exist within laundry distance, you're almost sure to find one further away. And it's a little easier to get admitted far away because colleges like a geographically diverse student body.

Now, in light of what you've read, what's best for you? Circle "Northeast," "South," "Midwest," or "West" on your *What I Want* list on p. 3. Before deciding, you might discuss it with your parent or counselor.

DECISION 7: Do I want a college offering many majors or a college that specializes?

Some colleges specialize. For example, Babson College focuses on business. Rose-Hulman specializes in engineering, and Julliard's thing is the performing arts. Don't tell your parents, but in Montreal, there's even a circus college (Cirque du Soleil). Specialty colleges are good choices if you're sure you know what you want to major in. Think about it; if you need a nose job, you're better off with a plastic surgeon than with your general all-purpose scalpel wielder.

Most colleges, however, offer a wide range of majors. These all-purpose institutions are ideal if you're not sure what you want to major in, and may also offer strong programs in specific fields. They're also good if you have a specific major in mind but want to attend a large college. Why? Because most specialty colleges are small.

Now, in light of what you've read, what's best for you? Circle "offer many majors" or "that specialize" on your *What I Want* list on p. 3. Before deciding, you might discuss it with your parent or counselor.

DECISION 8: Do I want a liberal, conservative, or moderate college?

At liberal colleges, the most popular shoes are Birkenstocks or Doc Martens. The most popular socks are no socks. The differences are more than superficial. At liberal colleges, most students support affirmative action, dislike corporate America, and think it's shallow to lust after a nice car. Fraternities and sororities don't exist or are widely dismissed as dens of elitism, racism, classism, sexism, and homophobia. Courses and extracurriculars are slanted toward save-the-environment themes, the contributions of minorities, and how America should redistribute additional wealth to the poor. There are many student activists and on-campus demonstrations.

At conservative colleges, few students act weird. Most think America is pretty good, and focus more on how to succeed within the system rather than on how to radically change it. At conservative colleges, most students oppose affirmative action. Fraternities, sororities, and traditional religion are often important, and attitudes toward sex (especially homosexuality) and drugs are conservative, although behavior may not be so conservative.

An Editorial: Why I generally recommend moderate institutions over liberal or conservative ones.

College is supposed to expose you to a wide range of perspectives. Unfortunately, you get a narrow range at many nonmoderate (liberal or conservative) institutions. Most lectures and reading assignments are slanted in one direction and students who disagree are made to feel uncomfortable, and perhaps risk a lower grade, so they usually sit silent. Professors who might not teach the party line get fired or aren't hired to begin with. Especially at liberal institutions, this is called *political correctness*.

Now, in light of what you've read, what's best for you? Circle "conservative," "moderate/diverse," or "liberal" on your *What I Want* list on p. 4. Before deciding, you might discuss it with your parent or counselor.

DECISION 9: Do I want to consider single-gender or single-race colleges?

On the plus side, students generally like them. Students form close bonds with each other, and feel a sense of empowerment around race and gender issues. People of their race or gender get to hold all the leadership positions. Although it may be because these colleges attract above-average students, graduates of these colleges do well in the job and graduate school market.

On the downside, you mainly get only your race's or gender's perspective in class discussions. Also, some graduates of single-gender or single-race colleges find it difficult to interact successfully with people not of their race or gender. One reason may simply be that their college provided them with less practice; single-sex or single-race colleges don't mirror the real world. Another reason is that these colleges can cause graduates to have a suspicious or angry attitude toward people not of their race or gender. This, of course, can make life more difficult professionally and personally.

Now, in light of what you've read, what's best for you? If you're interested in single-gender or single-race colleges, circle it on your *What I Want* list on p. 4. Before deciding, you might discuss it with your parent or counselor.

DECISION 10: Do I want to consider strongly religious colleges?

The undergraduate experience at many church-related colleges is not strongly religious. But at strongly religious colleges, your experience will be different. Most students will be of your faith. That can create close bonds and, if you're interested, help you find a mate of similar background. You'll be taking at least a few religion classes, and may be required to attend church. There may be less alcohol use, and probably will be less drug use. There are usually enforced rules that prohibit spending the night in a dorm room of a member of the opposite sex.

The disadvantages of single-gender and single-race colleges cited above may also apply to strongly religious colleges.

Now, in light of what you've read, what's best for you? If you're interested in a strongly religious college, circle it on your *What I Want* list on p. 4. Before deciding, you might discuss it with your parent or counselor.

DECISION 11: Do I care about the college's calendar?

Different colleges have different calendars. Does this matter to you? Read this chart:

CALENDAR	LENGTH OF EACH COURSE	# OF COURSES TAKEN BY GRADUATION
Quarter	10 weeks	60
Semester	15 weeks	40

I prefer the quarter system because you get to try out more courses and they're shorter. If you really like a course or a professor, you usually can take another, but if you can't stand the course, you're only stuck for ten weeks. The main reason to prefer a college that has a semester calendar is if you're concerned that midterms, finals, and term papers will come too quickly in a ten-week quarter.

The 4-1-4 calendar is sort of a compromise. The courses are halfway between semesters and quarters in length. (This gets confusing now.) Each year, you take 5 courses for 4 months, 1 course during a 1-month interterm, then 5 courses for 4 months. That's why it's called 4-1-4. Most students like the one-month interterm because you can focus, undistracted, on one hard or interesting course, and because fun courses are offered, for example, a "study" trip to Mexico. Or you can take an independent study. One student got interterm course credit for visiting six football stadiums and writing a paper about their differences.

The ultimate opportunity to focus is the block calendar. You take a total of 40 courses, just like at a semester-calendar college. The difference is that you take just one course at a time. Most students either love it or hate it. You'll love it if you'd enjoy immersing yourself in one subject for three and a half weeks, then moving to something else for three and a half weeks, and so on. It can be a nightmare for procrastinators and no picnic for science majors—try learning a semester's worth of organic chemistry in three and a half weeks.

The block calendar is offered only by a few colleges, notably Colorado College (that's not the University of Colorado) and Cornell College (the one in Iowa, not New York).

Now, in light of what you've read, what's best for you? Circle "quarter," "semester," "4-1-4," or "block" on your *What I Want* list on p. 4. Before deciding, you might discuss it with your parent or counselor.

DECISION 12: Do I want a college that offers a co-op program?

In a co-op program, you get course credit for doing a paid internship for a company or the government, under a professor's supervision.

Co-op is good because you get to apply classroom theory in a real-world setting. It helps you figure out what you want to be when you grow up. Your pay can help you to graduate from college loan-free, and co-op often leads to a good job after graduation. But because co-op yields little course credit for the many hours involved, co-op students often need an extra year to graduate.

Now, in light of what you've read, what's best for you? If you want to consider colleges with co-op programs, circle it on your *What I Want* list on p. 4. Before deciding, you might discuss it with your parent or a counselor.

DECISION 13: Do I need a college with extensive disability services?

The Americans with Disabilities Act requires all colleges receiving federal funds (nearly all colleges do) to provide services for the disabled. But some colleges offer much more than the minimum. Take, for example, services for the learning disabled. While most colleges provide tutoring, other colleges add note-takers, voice-input word processors, computers that scan printed material and then read it aloud, course books on tape, special advisors, and summer programs. Students with learning disabilities might want to consult *K & W Guide to Colleges for the Learning Disabled* (Princeton Review).

Now, in light of what you've read, what's best for you? If you want a college with extensive disability services, circle that item on your *What I Want* list on p. 4. Before deciding, you might want to discuss it with your parent or a counselor.

APPENDIX B
The Colleges

Listed here are 434 noteworthy colleges. Many other colleges, especially those close to home, can also be wise choices. If you don't know about your close-to-home colleges, see your counselor.

IMPORTANT: In all cases, Web addresses begin with *www*.

TWO-YEAR COLLEGES

Unless otherwise noted, all are small, away from big cities, and have students who mainly got Bs and Cs in high school.

NORTHEAST

Don't forget about your local colleges. (Need ideas? See your counselor.)

Becker $$$ v (suburban) MA *becker.edu* 508-791-9241 x445

Dean $$$ MA *dean.edu* 800-852-7702

Harcum $$$ w PA *harcum.edu* 800-345-2600

Keystone $$$ d PA *keystone.edu* 800-824-2764

Newbury $$$ v (suburban) MA *newbury.edu* 800-NEWBURY

Paul Smith's $$$ NY *paulsmiths.edu* 800-421-2605

Sage Junior of Albany $$$ (urban) NY *sage.edu* 888-VERY SAGE

Hartford College for Women $$$ (suburban) CT 800-582-6118

Landmark $$$$$ d (town) VT *landmarkcollege.org* 802-387-6718

Mitchell $$$$ d (incl. L.D. program fee) CT *mitchell.edu* 800-443-2811

CODES

$	1998–99 total estimated annual cost of under $12,000 per year
$$	1998–99 total estimated annual cost of $12,000–$18,000
$$$	1998–99 total estimated annual cost of $18,000–$24,000
$$$$	1998–99 total estimated annual cost of $24,000–$30,000
$$$$$	1998–99 total estimated annual cost of $30,000–$36,000

a African American/black	l liberal	T Tribal
c conservative	L living/learning program	t trimester calendar
d special learning	r strongly religious	v cooperative education
disability program	m men's	w women's
f 4-1-4- calendar	o block calendar	
(or similar calendar)	q quarter calendar	

SOUTH

Don't forget about your local colleges. (Need ideas? See your counselor.)
Brevard $$ d (town) NC *brevard.edu* 828-884-8300 (also offers 4-year
   programs)

MIDWEST

Don't forget about your local colleges (Need ideas? See your counselor.)
Sisseton-Wahpeton $ qT (no room & board) SD 605-698-3966
Vincennes $/$$ d IN *vinu.edu* 812-888-8888
Ricks $$ r ID *ricks.edu* 208-356-1026
Cottey $$ w MO *cottey.edu* 888-5-COTTEY
Lincoln $$$ IL *lincolncollege.edu* 800-569-0556
Waldorf $$$ v IA *waldorf.edu* 800-292-1903

WEST

Don't forget about your local colleges. (Need ideas? See your counselor.)
Dixie $ UT *dixie.edu* 888-GO 2 DIXIE
Yavapai $ AZ *yavapai.cc.az.us* 520-776-2150
Marymount $$$$ (suburban) CA *marymountpv.edu* 310-377-5501
Mount St. Mary's $$$$ (urban) CA *msmc.la.edu* 800-999-9893

FOUR-YEAR COLLEGES THAT OFFER MANY MAJORS

Unless otherwise noted, all have a politically/socially moderate or diverse student body, are not strongly religious, have men and women
students, run on a semester calendar, and do not offer co-op programs.

Mainly A students, small, Northeast, in or near a big city

Bryn Mawr $$$$$ w PA *brynmawr.edu* 800-BMC-1885
Columbia $$$$$ l NY *columbia.edu* 212-854-2522
Haverford $$$$$ PA *haverford.edu* 610-896-1350
Johns Hopkins $$$$$ fv MD *jhu.edu* 410-516-8171
Swarthmore $$$$$ l PA *swarthmore.edu* 610-328-8300
Wellesley $$$$$ w MA *wellesley.edu* 781-283-2270

For codes, see page 165.

Mainly A students, small, Northeast, town

Amherst $$$$$ t MA *amherst.edu* 413-542-2328

Bates College $$$$$ f ME *bates.edu* 207-786-6000

Bowdoin $$$$$ ME *bowdoin.edu* 207-725-3190

Middlebury $$$$$ f VT *middlebury.edu* 802-443-3000

Wesleyan $$$$$ lv CT *wesleyan.edu* 860-685-3000

Williams $$$$$ f MA *williams.edu* 413-597-2211

Mainly A students, small, South, in or near a big city

Rice $$$ TX *rice.edu* 800-527-OWLS

Mainly A students, small, South, town

Washington & Lee $$$ cf VA *wlu.edu* 540-463-8710

Mainly A students, small, Midwest, in or near a big city

U. of Chicago $$$$$ Lq IL *uchicago.edu* 773-702-8650

Mainly A students, small, Midwest, town

Carleton $$$$$ lt MN *carleton.edu* 800-995-2275

Oberlin $$$$$ lf OH *oberlin.edu* 800-622-OBIE

Mainly A students, small, West, in or near a big city

Claremont McKenna $$$$$ t CA *mckenna.edu* 909-621-8088

Pomona $$$$$ CA *pomona.edu* 909-621-8134

Reed $$$$$ l OR *reed.edu* 800-547-4750

Mainly A students, small, West, town

Deep Springs (a two-year college) $ lm 6 terms of 7 weeks CA *deep springs.edu* 619-872-2000

Mainly A students, large, Northeast, in or near a big city

Brown $$$$$ dlq RI *brown.edu* 401-863-2378

Georgetown $$$$$ d DC *georgetown.edu* 202-687-3600

For codes, see page 165.

Harvard **$$$$$** L MA fas.*harvard.edu* 617-495-1551

Massachusetts Institute of Technology **$$$$$** fv MA *web.mit.edu* 617-253-4791

Princeton **$$$$$** NJ *princeton.edu* 609-258-3060

Tufts **$$$$$** MA *tufts.edu* 617-627-3170

U. of Pennsylvania **$$$$$** f PA *upenn.edu* 215-898-7507

Yale **$$$$$** L CT *yale.edu* 203-432-9300

Mainly A students, large, Northeast, town

Cornell **$$$/$$$$** (public part) **$$$$$** (private part) dv NY *cornell.edu* 607-255-5241

Dartmouth **$$$$$** q NH *dartmouth.edu* 603-646-2875

Mainly A students, large, South, in or near a big city

Duke **$$$$$** NC *duke.edu* 919-684-3214

Mainly A students, large, South, town

College of William and Mary **$$/$$$** v VA *wm.edu* 757-221-4223

Mainly A students, large, Midwest, in or near a big city

Northwestern **$$$$$** qv IL *nwu.edu* 847-491-7271

Mainly A students, large, Midwest, town

U. of Notre Dame **$$$$** d IN *nd.edu* 219-631-7505

Mainly A students, large, West, in or near a big city

U. of California, Berkeley **$$/$$$$** dlv CA *berkeley.edu* 510-642-3175

U. of California, Los Angeles **$$/$$$$** dq CA *ucla.edu* 310-825-3101

Stanford **$$$$$** dq CA *stanford.edu* 650-723-2091

Mainly B to A students, small, Northeast, in or near a big city

Barnard **$$$$$** lwt NY *barnard.columbia.edu* 212-854-2014

Brandeis **$$$$$** lq MA *brandeis.edu* 800-622-0622

For codes, see page 165.

College of the Holy Cross $$$$$ r MA *holycross.edu* 800-442-2421
Sarah Lawrence $$$$$ l NY *slc.edu* 800-888-2858
Trinity $$$$$ CT *trincoll.edu* 860-297-2180
Union $$$$$ t NY *union.edu* 518-388-6112

Mainly B to A students, small, Northeast, town
Grove City $$ c PA *gcc.edu* 724-458-2100
St. Mary's College of Maryland $$/$$$ MD *smcm.edu* 800-492-7181
Bard College $$$$$ lf NY *bard.edu* 914-758-7472
Bucknell University $$$$$ c PA *bucknell.edu* 717-524-1101
Colby $$$$$ f ME *colby.edu* 800-723-3032
Colgate $$$$$ NY *colgate.edu* 315-228-7401
Connecticut College $$$$$ CT *camel.conncoll.edu* 860-439-2202
Franklin & Marshall $$$$$ PA *fandm.edu* 717-291-3953
Gettysburg $$$$$ PA *gettysburg.edu* 800-431-0803
Hamilton $$$$$ NY *hamilton.edu* 800-843-2655
Lafayette $$$$$ f PA *lafayette.edu* 610-250-5100
Mount Holyoke $$$$$ wf PA *mtholyoke.edu* 413-538-2023
St. John's $$$$$ MD *sjca.edu* 800-727-9238
Simon's Rock College of Bard $$$$$ MA *simons-rock.edu*
    800-235-7186
Smith $$$$$ w MA *smith.edu* 413-585-2500
Vassar $$$$$ NY *vassar.edu* 914-437-7300

Mainly B to A students, small, South, in or near a big city
New College of the U. of South Florida $$ lf FL *newcollege.usf.edu*
    941-359-4269
Trinity $$$ TX *trinity.edu* 800-TRINITY
Rhodes $$$$ TN *rhodes.edu* 800-844-5969
U. of Richmond $$$$ c VA *richmond.edu* 800-700-1662
Wake Forest $$$$ NC *wfu.edu* 336-758-5201

For codes, see page 165.

Mainly B to A students, small, South, town

Mary Washington $$ v VA *mwc.edu* 800-468-5614

U. of the South $$$$ c TN *sewanee.edu* 800-522-2234

Davidson $$$$$ cr NC *davidson.edu* 800-768-0380

Mainly B to A students, small, Midwest, in or near a big city

Case Western Reserve $$$$ qv OH *cwru.edu* 216-368-4450

Colorado College $$$$ lo CO *cc.colorado.edu* 800-542-7214

Macalester $$$$ lf MN *macalester.edu* 800-231-7974

Mainly B to A students, small, Midwest, town

U. of Minnesota-Morris $$/$$$ q MN *mrs.umn.edu* 800-992-8863

Grinnell $$$$ l IA *grin.edu* 800-247-0113

Kenyon $$$$$ OH *kenyon.edu* 800-848-2468

Mainly B to A students, small, West, in or near a big city

Occidental $$$$$ l CA *oxy.edu* 800-825-5262

Mainly B to A students, large, Northeast, in or near a big city

McGill University $$ (Canadians)/$$ (Non-Canadians) CANADA
mcgill.ca 514-398-3910

U. of Toronto $$ (Canadians)/$$ (Non-Canadians) CANADA
utoronto.ca 416-978-2190

College of New Jersey $$/$$$ NJ *tcnj.edu* 800-624-0967

Rutgers $$/$$$ NJ *rutgers.edu* 732-932-4636

Boston College $$$$$ MA *bc.edu* 800-360-2522

Carnegie Mellon $$$$$ v PA *cmu.edu* 412-268-2082

New York U. $$$$$ NY *nyu.edu* 212-998-4500

U. of Rochester $$$$$ NY *rochester.edu* 888-822-2256

State U. of New York at Buffalo: $$/$$$ NY *buffalo.edu*
716-645-6900

For codes, see page 165.

170

Mainly B to A students, large, Northeast, town

Queen's University **$$** (Canadians)/**$$** (Non-Canadians) (CANADA)
 queensu.ca 613-545-2218

State U. of New York at Binghamton **$$/$$** NY *binghamton.edu*
 607-777-2171

State U. of New York, College at Geneseo **$$/$$** NY *geneseo.edu*
 716-245-5571

Pennsylvania State U., Main Campus **$$/$$$** v PA *psu.edu*
 814-865-5471

U. of Vermont **$$/$$$$** vd VT *uvm.edu* 802-656-3370

Lehigh **$$$$$** v PA *lehigh.edu* 610-758-3100

Mainly B to A students, large, South, in or near a big city

U. of Texas at Austin **$/$$** TX *utexas.edu* 512-475-7440

U. of North Carolina, Chapel Hill **$/$$$** NC *unc.edu* 919-966-3621

Emory **$$$$$** GA *emory.edu* 800-727-6036

Tulane **$$$$$** LA *tulane.edu* 800-873-9283

Vanderbilt **$$$$$** TN *vanderbilt.edu* 615-322-2561

Mainly B to A students, large, South, town

U. of Virginia **$$/$$$** d VA *virginia.edu* 804-982-3200

Mainly B to A students, large, Midwest, in or near a big city

U. of Wisconsin, Madison **$/$$$** v WI *wisc.edu* 608-262-3961

University of Michigan **$$/$$$$** dtv MI *umich.edu* 734-764-7433

Washington U. **$$$$$** v MO *wustl.edu* 800-638-0700

Mainly B to A students, large, Midwest, town

Truman State **$/$$** MO *truman.edu* 660-785-4114

Miami U. **$$/$$$** v OH *muohio.edu* 513-529-2531

For codes, see page 165.

Mainly B to A students, large, West, in or near a big city

U. of California, San Diego **$$/$$$$** q CA *infopath.ucsd.edu*
    619-534-4831

Mainly B to A students, large, West, town

California Polytechnic State U., San Luis Obispo **$$/$$$** dqv CA
    calpoly.edu 805-756-2311
U. of California, Davis **$$/$$$** dq CA *ucdavis.edu* 530-752-2971

Many B– students, small, Northeast, in or near a big city

Don't forget about your local colleges. (Need ideas? See your counselor.)
Trent **$$** (Canadians)/**$$** (Non-Canadians) l CANADA *trentu.ca*
    705-748-1215
American International **$$$** d MA *aic.edu* 800-242-3142
Mercyhurst **$$$** tvd PA *mercyhurst.edu* 800-825-1926
Catholic U. of America **$$$$** r DC *cua.edu* 202-319-5305
Clark **$$$$$** l MA *clarku.edu* 508-793-7431
Curry **$$$$** qd MA *curry.edu* 800-669-0686
Iona **$$$$** fd NY *iona.edu* 914-633-2502
Loyola **$$$$** MD *loyola.edu* 800-221-9107
Muhlenberg **$$$$** PA *muhlenberg.edu* 610-821-3200
New England College **$$$$** qd NH *nec.edu* 603-428-2223
Wagner **$$$$** NY *wagner.edu* 718-390-3411
Drew **$$$$$** NJ *drew.edu* 973-408-3739
Eugene Lang **$$$$$** I NY *newschool.edu* 212-229-5665
Goucher **$$$$$** MD *goucher.edu* 800-GOUCHER
Simmons **$$$$$** w MA *simmons.edu* 617-521-2051
Skidmore **$$$$$** NY *skidmore.edu* 800-867-6007

Many B– students, small, Northeast, town

Don't forget about your local colleges. (Need ideas? See your counselor.)
Acadia **$$** (Canadians)/**$$** (Non-Canadians) CANADA *acadiau.ca*
    902-585-1222

For codes, see page 165.

Mount Allison $$ (Canadians)/$$ (Non-Canadians) CANADA *mta.ca*
    506-364-2269

Ramapo $$/$$ v NJ *ramapo.edu* 201-529-6451

Pennsylvania State at Erie, Behrend College $$/$$$ PA *psu.edu*
    814-898-6100

College of the Atlantic $$$$ lqv ME *coa.edu* 800-528-0025

Siena $$$ crq NY *siena.edu* 800-45-SIENA

Southern Vermont $$$ d VT *svc.edu* 802-442-5427 x6304

Elizabethtown $$$$ PA *etown.edu* 717-361-1400

Goddard $$$$ lv VT *goddard.edu* 800-468-4888

Gordon $$$$ cr MA *gordonc.edu* 800-343-1379

Quinniapiac $$$$ CT *quinnipiac.edu* 203-281-8600

St. Anselm's $$$$ NH *anselm.edu* 888-4ANSELM

St. Joseph's $$$$ v PA *sju.edu* 610-660-1300

St. Michael's $$$$ VT *smcvt.edu* 800-762-8000

Salve Regina $$$$ RI *salve.edu* 888-GO-SALVE

Susquehanna $$$$ c PA *susqu.edu* 800-326-9672

U. of New England $$$$ dv ME *une.edu* 800-477-4UNE

Ursinus $$$$ PA *ursinus.edu* 610-409-3200

Washington College $$$$ MD *washcoll.edu* 800-422-1782

Western Maryland $$$$ MD *wmdc.edu* 800-638-5005

Alfred $$$$$ qv NY *alfred.edu* 800-541-9229

Allegheny $$$$ lq PA *alleg.edu* 800-521-5293

Bennington $$$$$ l VT *bennington.edu* 800-833-6845

Dickinson $$$$$ PA *dickinson.edu* 800-644-1773

Hampshire $$$$$ lf MA *hampshire.edu* 413-582-5471

Hartwick $$$$$ t NY *hartwick.edu* 607-431-4150

Hobart & William Smith $$$$$ t NY *hws.edu* 800-245-0100

Manhattanville $$$$$ NY *manhattanville.edu* 800-328-4553

Marlboro $$$$$ t VT *marlboro.edu* 802-257-4333 x237

St. Lawrence $$$$$ NY *stlawu.edu* 800-285-1856

Wheaton $$$$$ MA *wheatonma.edu* 800-394-6003

For codes, see page 165.

Many B– students, small, South, in or near a big city

Don't forget about your local colleges. (Need ideas? See your counselor.)

The Citadel **$/$$** c SC *citadel.edu* 800-868-1842

Hendrix **$$** t AR *hendrix.edu* 800-277-9017

Xavier U. of Louisiana **$$** av LA *xula.edu* 504-483-7388

Birmingham-Southern College **$$$** cf AL *bsc.edu* 800-523-5793

Millsaps **$$$** MS *millsaps.edu* 800-352-1050

Morehouse **$$$** amv GA *morehouse.edu* 800-851-1254

Our Lady of the Lake **$$$** v TX *ollusa.edu* 210-434-6711 x314

Samford **$$** crfv AL *samford.edu* 800-888-7218

Spelman **$$** wa GA *spelman.edu* 404-681-3643 x2188

St. Edward's **$$$** v TX *stedwards.edu* 512-448-8500

Thomas More **$$$** cv KY *thomasmore.edu* 800-825-4557

Transylvania **$$$** f KY *transy.edu* 800-872-6798

U. of Dallas **$$$** cr TX *udallas.edu* 800-628-6999

Wofford **$$$** cfv SC *wofford.edu* 864-597-4130

Agnes Scott **$$$$** wt GA *agnescott.edu* 800-868-8602

Eckerd **$$$$** f FL *eckerd.edu* 800-456-9009

Furman **$$$$** crtv SC *furman.edu* 864-294-2034

Guilford **$$$** NC *guilford.edu* 800-992-7759

Hollins **$$$$** wf VA *hollins.edu* 800-456-9595

Oglethorpe **$$$$** v GA *oglethorpe.edu* 800-428-4484

Rollins **$$$$$** f FL *rollins.edu* 407-646-2161

Many B– students, small, South, town

Don't forget about your local colleges. (Need ideas? See your counselor.)

College of the Ozarks **$** df MO *cofo.edu* 800-222-0525

Berea **$** f KY *berea.edu* 800-326-5948

U. of Montevallo **$/$$** AL *montevallo.edu* 205-665-6030

U. of North Carolina, Asheville **$/$$** NC *unca.edu* 704-251-6481

Winthrop **$/$$** v SC *winthrop.edu* 800-763-0230

Flagler **$$** FL *flagler.edu* 800-504-4208 x220

Lenoir-Rhyne **$$** c NC *lrc.edu* 800-277-5721

For codes, see page 165.

Austin $$$ f TX *austinc.edu* 800-442-5363

Catawba $$$ NC *catawba.edu* 704-637-4402

Centre $$$ f KY *centre.edu* 800-423-6236

Davis & Elkins $$$ dv WV *dne.edu* 800-624-3157

Elon $$$ fv NC *elon.edu* 800-334-8448

Emory & Henry $$$ VA *ehc.edu* 800-848-5493

Presbyterian $$$ SC *presby.edu* 800-476-7272

Southwestern $$$ TX *southwestern.edu* 800-252-3166

St. Andrew's Presbyterian $$$ f NC *sapc.edu* 800-763-0198

Warren Wilson $$$ l NC *warren-wilson.edu* 800-934-3536

Hampden-Sydney $$$$ cm VA *hsc.edu* 800-755-0733

Lynn $$$$ d FL 800-544-8055

Randolph-Macon Woman's College $$$$ w VA *rmwc.edu*
    800-745-7692

Sweet Briar $$$$ cwf VA *sbc.edu* 800-381-6142

West Virginia Wesleyan $$$$ df WV *wvwc.edu* 304-473-8510

Many B– students, small, Midwest, in or near a big city

Don't forget about your local colleges. (Need ideas? See your counselor.)

Alverno $$ wv WI *alverno.edu* 800-933-3401

Calvin $$$ crfv MI *calvin.edu* 800-668-0122

Concordia $$$ q MI *ccaa.edu* 800-253-0680

Nebraska Wesleyan $$$ cq NE *nebrwesleyan.edu* 402-465-2218

Ohio Dominican $$$ OH *odc.edu* 800-854-2670

Oral Roberts $$$ cr OK *oru.edu* 918-495-6518

St. Norbert $$$ v WI *snc.edu* 800-236-4878

Stephens $$$ w MO *stephens.edu* 800-876-7207

U. of Tulsa $$$ OK *utulsa.edu* 800-331-3050

Wheaton $$$ cr IL *wheaton.edu* 630-752-5011

William Jewell $$$ c MO *jewell.edu* 800-753-7009

Kalamazoo $$$$ qv MI *kzoo.edu* 800-253-3602

Lake Forest $$$$ IL *lfc.edu* 800-828-4751

U. of Denver $$$$ dqv CO *du.edu* 303-871-3373

For codes, see page 165.

Wittenberg U. $$$$ t OH *wittenberg.edu* 800-677-7558

Many B– students, small, Midwest, town

Don't forget about your local colleges. (Need ideas? See your counselor.)

Oglala Lakota $ T (no room & board) SD 605-455-2321 x236

Sinte Gleska $ T (no room & board) SD 605-747-2263

Shimer $$ v (no board) IL *shimer.edu* 800-215-7173

Adrian $$$ v MI *adrian.edu* 800-877-2246

Alma $$$ f MI *alma.edu* 800-321-ALMA

Baker U. $$$ f KS *bakeru.edu* 800-873-4282

Barat $$$ d IL *barat.edu* 847-295-4260

Buena Vista $$$ f IA *bvu.edu* 800-383-9600

Carroll $$$ v MT *carroll.edu* 800-99-ADMIT

Carroll $$$ WI *cc.edu* 800-CARROLL

Hanover $$$ f IN *hanover.edu* 800-213-2178

Hillsdale $$$ cq MI *hillsdale.edu* 517-437-7341 x2327

Loras $$$ d IA *loras.edu* 800-24-LORAS

Muskingum $$$ d OH *muskingum.edu* 800-752-6082

Rocky Mountain $$$ v MT *rocky.edu* 800-877-6259

St. John's/St. Benedict $$$ mwf MN *csbsju.edu* 800-24-JOHNS

U. of Evansville $$$ cv IN *evansville.edu* 812-479-2468

Valparaiso $$$ crv IN *valpo.edu* 219-464-5011

Wartburg $$$ f IA *wartburg.edu* 800-772-2085

Westminster College $$$ d MO *wcmo.edu* 800-475-3361

Albion $$$$ MI *albion.edu* 800-858-6770

Antioch $$$$ lqv OH *college,antioch.edu* 937-767-6400 x6559

Beloit $$$$ WI *beloit.edu* 608-363-2500

Butler $$$$ IN *butler.edu* 888-940-8100

College of Wooster $$$$ OH *wooster.edu* 800-877-9905

Cornell $$$$ o IA *cornell-iowa.edu* 800-747-1112

Denison $$$$$ f OH *denison.edu* 800-DENISON

DePauw $$$$ f IN *depauw.edu* 800-447-2495

Earlham $$$$ lq IN *earlham.edu* 800-327-5426

For codes, see page 165.

176

Gustavus Adolphus $$$$ fv MN *gac.edu* 800-GUSTAVUS
Hiram $$$$ q OH *hiram.edu* 800-362-5280
Illinois Wesleyan $$$$ f IL *iwu.edu* 800-332-2498
Knox $$$$ t IL *knox.edu* 800-678-KNOX
Lawrence $$$$ t WI *lawrence.edu* 800-227-0982
Ohio Wesleyan $$$$ OH *owu.edu* 800-922-8953
Ripon $$$$ WI *ripon.edu* 800-947-4766
St. Olaf $$$$ f MN *stolaf.edu* 507-646-3025
Wabash $$$$ cm IN *wabash.edu* 800-345-5385

Many B– students, small, West, in or near a big city

Don't forget about your local colleges. (Need ideas? See your counselor.)
Gonzaga $$$$ WA *gonzaga.edu* 800-322-2584
Lewis & Clark $$$$ lq OR *lclark.edu* 800-444-4111
Loyola Marymount $$$$ CA *lmu.edu* 800-LMU-INFO
Mills $$$$ lvw CA *mills.edu* 800-87-MILLS
Pacific Lutheran $$$$ fv WA *plu.edu* 800-274-6758
Santa Clara $$$$ qv CA *scu.edu* 408-554-4700
St. Mary's College of California $$$$ f CA *stmarys-ca.edu*
   800-800-4SMC
U. of Portland $$$$ v OR *uofport.edu* 503-283-7147
Puget Sound $$$$ v WA *ups.edu* 800-396-7191
U. of San Diego $$$$ r CA *acusd.edu* 619-260-4506
Pepperdine $$$$$ cr CA *pepperdine.edu* 310-456-4392
Pitzer $$$$$ lv CA *pitzer.edu* 800-748-9371 (in-state) 800-749-9371
   (out-of-state)
Scripps $$$$$ w CA *scrippscol.edu* 800-770-1333
St. John's $$$$$ NM *sjcsf.edu* 800-331-5232
Willamette U. $$$$$ OR *willamette.edu* 503-370-6303

Many B– students, small, West, town

Don't forget about your local colleges. (Need ideas? See your counselor.)
Ft. Lewis $ tv CO *fortlewis.edu* 970-247-7184

For codes, see page 165.

Grand Canyon $$ r AZ *grand-canyon.edu* 800-800-9776

Albertson $$$ ID *acofi.edu* 800-AC-IDAHO

College of Santa Fe $$$ NM *csf.edu* 505-475-6133

Hawaii Pacific $$$ fv HI *hpu.edu* 800-669-4724

Linfield $$$$ f OR *linfield.edu* 800-640-2887

Thomas Aquinas $$$$ c CA *thomasaquinas.edu* 800-634-9797

Westmont $$$$ cr CA *westmont.edu* 805-565-6200 x6003

Whitman $$$$ WA *whitman.edu* 509-527-5176

Whitworth $$$$ cfrv WA *whitworth.edu* 800-533-4668

Redlands $$$$$ fv CA *redlands.edu* 800-455-5064

Many B– students, large, Northeast, in or near a big city

Don't forget about your local colleges. (Need ideas? See your counselor.)

State U. of New York, Albany $$/$$$ NY *albany.edu* 518-442-5435

U. of Maryland, College Park $$/$$$ v MD *uga.umd.edu* 800-422-5867

Adelphi $$$ d NY *adelphi.edu* 800-ADELPHI

Hofstra $$$ df NY *hofstra.edu* 800-HOFSTRA

Howard $$$ a DC *howard.edu* 202-806-2900

Duquesne $$$$ v PA *duq.edu* 800-456-0590

Fordham $$$$ NY *fordham.edu* 800-FORDHAM

Long Island U. Post campus $$$$ dv NY: *liu.edu* 800-LIU-PLAN

American U. $$$$$ dv DC *american.edu* 202-885-6000

Boston U. $$$$$ dv MA *bu.edu* 617-353-2300

Syracuse $$$$$ v NY *syr.edu* 315-443-3611

Villanova $$$$$ PA *villanova.edu* 800-338-7927

Many B– students, large, Northeast, town

Don't forget about your local colleges. (Need ideas? See your counselor.)

Indiana U. of Pennsylvania $/$$ v PA *iup.edu* 800-442-6830

Millersville U. of Pennsylvania $/$$ fv PA *millersv.edu* 800-MU-ADMIT

Shippensburg U. of Pennsylvania $/$$ PA *ship.edu* 800-822-8028

U. of Maine, Orono $$/$$ v ME *umaine.edu* 207-581-1561

For codes, see page 165.

State U. of New York at Stony Brook **$$/$$$** NY *sunysb.edu*
    516-632-6868

U. of Connecticut **$$/$$$** v CT *uconn.edu* 860-486-3137

U. of Delaware **$$/$$$** fv DE *udel.edu* 302-831-8123

U. of Massachusetts, Amherst **$$/$$$** MA *umass.edu*
    413-545-0222

U. of New Hampshire **$$/$$$** NH *unh.edu* 603-862-1360

Ithaca **$$$$** NY *ithaca.edu* 800-429-4274

Many B– students, large, South, in or near a big city

Don't forget about your local colleges. (Need ideas? See your counselor.)

College of Charleston **$/$$** v SC *cofc.edu* 843-953-5670

Florida State **$/$$** v FL *fsu.edu* 850-644-6200

Louisiana State **$/$$** v LA *lsu.edu* 504-388-1175

U. of Kentucky **$/$$** v KY *uky.edu* 606-257-2000

U. of South Carolina-Columbia **$/$$** v SC *sc.edu* 800-868-5USC

U. of Tennessee, Knoxville **$/$$** v KY *utk.edu* 423-974-2184

U. of Alabama (Tuscaloosa) **$/$$** v AL *ua.edu* 800-933-BAMA

U. of Florida **$/$$** dv FL *ufl.edu* 352-392-1365

Baylor University **$$** cr TX *baylor.edu* 800-BAYLORU

Texas Christian **$$$** c TX *tcu.edu* 800-TCU-3764

Southern Methodist **$$$$** cv TX *smu.edu* 800-323-0672

U. of Miami **$$$$$** FL *miami.edu* 305-284-4323

Many B– students, large, South, town

Don't forget about your local colleges. (Need ideas? See your counselor.)

Georgia Southern **$/$** cqv GA *gasou.edu* 912-681-5531

U. of Mississippi **$/$** MS *olemiss.edu* 601-232-7226

Appalachian State **$/$$** NC 704-262-2120

Auburn U. **$/$$** v AL *auburn.edu* 205-844-4080

Austin Peay **$/$$** TN *apsu.edu* 615-648-7661

Clemson **$/$$** v SC *clemson.edu* 803-656-2287

Texas A & M **$/$$** cv TX *tamu.edu* 409-845-3741

For codes, see page 165.

U. of Arkansas, Main Campus $/$$ v AR 800-377-UOFA
U. of Georgia $/$$ dqv GA *uga.edu* 706-542-2112
West Virginia U. $/$$ v WV *arc.wvu.edu* 800-344-9881
Virginia Polytechnic Institute & State U. $/$$$ v VA *vt.edu*
  703-231-6267
James Madison $$/$$ VA *jmu.edu* 703-568-6147

Many B– students, large, Midwest, in or near a big city

Don't forget about your local colleges. (Need ideas? See your counselor.)
Fort Hays State $/$$ d KS *fhsu.edu* 785-628-4222
U. of Iowa $/$$ v IA *uiowa.edu* 800-553-4692
U. of Kansas $/$$ v KS *ukans.edu* 785-864-3911
U. of Missouri, Columbia $/$$ v MO *missouri.edu* 573-882-7786
U. of Nebraska, Lincoln $/$$ v NE *unl.edu* 800-742-8800
U. of Oklahoma $/$$ v OK *ou.edu* 800-234-6868
Colorado State $/$$$ dv CO *colostate.edu* 970-491-6909
Michigan State $/$$$ v MI *msu.edu* 517-355-8332
Ohio State $/$$$ dqv OH *ohio-state.edu* 614-292-3980
U. of Minnesota, Twin Cities $/$$$ qv MN *umn.edu* 800-752-1000
University of Waterloo $$ (Canadians)/$$ (Non-Canadians) tv
  CANADA *uwaterloo.ca* 519-888-4567 x2265
Western Michigan $$/$$ v MI *wmich.edu* 800-400-4WMU
U. of Illinois, Urbana-Champaign $$/$$$ v IL *illinois.edu* 217-333-0302
U. of Colorado at Boulder $$/$$$$ dv CO *colorado.edu* 303-492-6301
Bradley $$$ v IL *bradley.edu* 800-447-6460
Creighton $$$ c NE *creighton.edu* 402-280-2703
De Paul $$$ dq IL *depaul.edu* 800-4DEPAUL
U. of Dayton $$$ v OH *udayton.edu* 800-837-7433
U. of St. Thomas $$$ f MN *stthomas.edu* 800-328-6819 x26150
Drake $$$$ v IA *drake.edu* 800-44-DRAKE
Marquette $$$$ WI *marquette.edu* 800-222-6544

For codes, see page 165.

Many B– students, large, Midwest, town

Don't forget about your local colleges. (Need ideas? See your counselor.)

Ohio U. **$/$$** qv OH *ohiou.edu* 740-593-4100

Southern Illinois U. **$/$$** dv IL *siu.edu* 618-536-4405

U. of Wisconsin, Eau Claire **$/$$** f WI *uwec.edu* 715-836-5415

U. of Wyoming **$/$$** v WY *uwyo.edu* 800-DIAL-WYO

Purdue **$/$$$** v IN *purdue.edu* 765-494-4600

Indiana U. **$$/$$$** v IN *indiana.edu* 812-855-0661

Many B– students, large, West, in or near a big city

Don't forget about your local colleges. (Need ideas? See your counselor.)

Brigham Young University **$** crfv UT *byu.edu* 801-378-2539

Arizona State **$/$$** dv AZ *asu.edu* 602-965-7788

U. of Arizona **$/$$** dv AZ *arizona.edu* 520-621-3237

U. of British Columbia **$** (Canadians)/ **$$** (Non-Canadians) CANADA
  ubc.ca 604-822-9325

U. of Nevada, Las Vegas **$/$$** dv NV *unlv.edu* 800-334-UNLV

U. of New Mexico **$/$$** v NM *unm.edu* 505-277-2446

U. of Utah **$/$$** qv UT *utah.edu* 800-444-8638

U. of Oregon **$/$$$** dq OR *uoregon.edu* 541-346-3201

U. of Washington **$/$$$** qv WA *washington.edu* 206-543-9686

U. of Hawaii at Manoa **$$/$$$** v HI *hawaii.edu* 808-956-8975

U. of California, Santa Barbara **$$/$$$** qv CA *ucsb.edu* 805-893-2485

U. of Southern California **$$$$$** dv CA *usc.edu* 213-740-1111

Many B– students, large, West, town

Don't forget about your local colleges. (Need ideas? See your counselor.)

Evergreen State **$/$$** lqv WA *evergreen.edu* 360-866-6000 x6170

University of Idaho **$/$$** v ID *uidaho.edu* 208-885-6326

University of Montana **$/$$** v MT *umt.edu* 800-462-8636

Western Washington **$/$$** qv WA *wwu.edu* 360-650-3440 x3443

California State Stanislaus **$/$$$** fv CA *csustan.edu* 209-667-3070

Humboldt State University **$/$$$** lqv CA *humboldt.edu* 707-826-4402

For codes, see page 165.

Oregon State **$/$$$** qv OR *osu.orst.edu* 800-291-4192
Sonoma State **$$/$$$** d CA *sonoma.edu* 707-664-2778
U. of California, Santa Cruz **$$/$$$** lq CA *ucsc.edu* 408-459-2131

FOUR-YEAR COLLEGES THAT SPECIALIZE IN CERTAIN MAJORS

NOTE: These colleges focus just on a few popular careers. Other career-specific colleges and technical institutes specialize in such careers as nursing, photography, and culinary arts (chef). To find out more about these, check with your counselor or with a local two-year college.

Military Institutions

United States Air Force Academy **$0** c CO *usafa.af.mil* 800-443-9266
United States Coast Guard Academy **$0** c CT *cga.edu* 800-883-8724
United States Military Academy **$0** c NY *usma.edu* 914-938-4041
United States Merchant Marine Academy **$0** c NY *usmma.edu*
    516-773-5391
United States Naval Academy **$0** c MD *nadn.navy.mil* 800-638-9156

Institutions Specializing in
Engineering and Physical Sciences

(Unless otherwise noted, all are four-year, small, suburban or urban, and require a solid B average.)
Don't forget about your local colleges. (Need ideas? See your counselor.)
Montana Tech **$/$$** cq MT *mtech.edu* 800-445-TECH
Georgia Institute of Technology (large, mainly A students) **$/$$$** qv
    GA *gatech.edu* 404-894-4154
Cooper Union (mainly A students) **$$** NY *cooper.edu* 212-353-4120
California Maritime Academy **$$/$$$** c CA *csum.edu* 800-561-1945
Michigan Technological U. **$$/$$$** qv MI *mtu.edu* 906-487-2335
U. of Missouri, Rolla **$$/$$$** v MO *umr.edu* 800-522-0938
Colorado School of Mines **$$/$$$$** v CO *mines.edu* 800-446-9488
Kettering University **$$$** tv MI *kettering.edu* 800-955-4464
California Institute of Technology (all A students) **$$$$** t CA
    caltech.edu 800-568-8324

For codes, see page 165.

Clarkson **$$$$** v NY *clarkson.edu* 315-268-6479

Rose-Hulman Institute of Technology **$$$$** cq IN *rose-hulman.edu*
    812-877-8213

Worcester Polytechnic Institute **$$$$** v 4 7-week terms MA
    wpi.edu 508-831-5286

Harvey Mudd (mainly A students) **$$$$$** CA *hmc.edu* 909-621-8011

Massachusetts Institute of Technology (mainly A students, large)
    $$$$$ fv MA *web.mit.edu* 617-253-4791

Rensselaer (mid-sized, town) **$$$$$** v NY *rpi.edu* 518-276-6216

Institutions Specializing in Business

(All are four-year, small, in or near a big city, accept some B– or even C+
students, and use a quarter calendar.)
Don't forget about your local colleges. (Need ideas? See your counselor.)
Bentley College **$$$$** MA *bentley.edu* 781-891-2244

Bryant College **$$$$** RI *bryant.edu* 800-622-7001

Babson College (mainly B students or better) **$$$$$** MA *babson.edu*
    800-488-3696

Institutions Specializing in the Visual Arts

(Unless otherwise noted, all are four-year, small, in or near a big city,
take about half of applicants with special emphasis on the portfolio.)
Don't forget about your local colleges. (Need ideas? See your counselor.)
North Carolina School of the Arts **$/$$** t NC *ncarts.edu* 910-770-3291

Cooper Union (mainly A students) **$$** NY *cooper.edu* 212-353-4120

Fashion Institute of Technology (easier admission) **$$/$$** NY
    fitnyc.suny.edu 800-GO-TO-FIT

Art Center College of Design (no room & board) **$$$** lt CA
    artcenter.edu 626-396-2373

Kansas City Art Institute **$$$$** MO *kcai.edu* 800-522-5224

Maryland Institute College of Art **$$$$** l MD *mica.edu* 410-225-2222

School of the Art Institute of Chicago (easier admission) **$$$$** IL
    artic.edu/saic 800-232-SAIC

For codes, see page 165.

Otis College of Art & Design (easier admission) $$$$ CA
   otisarts.edu 800-527-OTIS

Parsons School of Design $$$$$ l NY *parsons.edu* 800-252-0852

Rhode Island School of Design $$$$$ lf RI *risd.edu* 800-364-RISD

Institutions Specializing in the Performing Arts

*(Unless otherwise noted, all are four-year, small, suburban or urban, take
about half of applicants with special emphasis on performing ability.)*

Don't forget about your local colleges. (Need ideas? See your counselor.)

Curtis Institute of Music (most selective) (No room & board) $ PA
   curtis.edu 215-893-5262

Purchase College, State U. of NY $$/$$$ lq NY *purchase.edu*
   914-251-6300

California Institute of the Arts $$$ lt (town) CA *calarts.edu*
   800-292-ARTS (instate) 800-545-ARTS out-of-state

Cleveland Institute of Music $$$ q OH *cim.edu* 216-795-3107

Columbia College (easier admission) $$$ IL *colum.edu*
   312-344-7130

Julliard (most selective) $$$ q NY *julliard.edu* 212-799-5000 x223

Berklee College of Music $$$$ MA *berklee.edu* 800-421-0084

Eastman School of Music (very selective) $$$$$ NY
   rochester.edu/eastman 716-274-1060

Manhattan School of Music $$$$$ q NY *msmnyc.edu*
   212-749-2802, x2

Mannes College of Music $$$$$ q NY *mannes.edu* 212-580-0210 x246

New England Conservatory $$$$$ q MA *newenglandconservatory.edu*
   617-262-1120 x430

Oberlin Conservatory $$$$$ f OH 440-775-8413

NOTES

   1. A "small" college is defined as under 5,000 full-time-equivalent
   undergraduates.

   2. Cost is defined as the published cost of one year's tuition, fees, room

For codes, see page 165.

and board for the 1998–99 school year plus an estimate of the average amount actually spent on books, spending money, and travel. Where two prices are given, the first is for in-state residents, the second, for out-of-staters. Contact each school for current figures. Remember that some families can get significant financial aid. (See Chapter 4.)

3. The decision to describe a college as "liberal," "conservative," or "strongly religious" was made by synthesizing the input of counselors, college guides, and the author. Colleges marked as liberal or conservative are those viewed as unmistakably so. Many other colleges, including most of the nation's hardest-to-get-into colleges, are generally liberal in tone.

4. Honors programs are not individually identified because most colleges have them. Some institutions known for their high-quality honors programs are: the Universities of Delaware, Georgia, Indiana, Maryland, Michigan, North Carolina, Ohio State, Oregon, Penn State, South Carolina, Texas, Utah, Virginia, Washington, and the College of William & Mary. You can quickly assess the quality of any college's honors program by using the approach on p. 15.

APPENDIX C
College Planning Calendar

Junior Year of High School

FALL & WINTER

✓ Take a challenging course schedule and get good grades. When in doubt, choose an honors rather than a regular class. This year and the first half of next year are the most important for college admissions.

✓ Register in early September for the PSAT in October.

✓ Be sure you have a social security card. It's required for college applications.

✓ To get the maximum financial aid, money for college should be saved in the parent's name, not the student's. Where possible, family expenses should be paid with money that already is in the student's name. Capital gains should be taken by December 31 of your junior year. If your parents only put money aside for retirement in some years, the best time to do it is by December 31 of your junior year.

SPRING

✓ Plan to take a strong academic load during your senior year. Colleges look closely at this.

✓ Select a tentative major (See pp. 197–198 for how.)

✓ If you think you'll be applying Early Decision or Early Action, sign up for the May administration of the SAT I or ACT.

✓ In June, if aiming for a hard-to-get-into college, take three SAT II exams: writing, math, and your best other subject. (Forget about the latter if you took the SAT II: Biology at the end of your sophomore year.)

✓ Develop a tentative list of colleges by completing Chapter 1 and 2 in this book. Involve your parents, but don't let them dominate.

✓ If you're a "superstar," an "underrepresented" minority, or know that your family will not qualify for much financial aid, consider investigating private scholarships. A good free scholarship search service is at *scholarships.salliemae.com*. If you don't have Web access, you can access the same service for $20 by calling 800-462-2743.

✓ Consider taking Advanced Placement exams.

✓ Create a filing system for college materials.

SUMMER

✓ Find or explore a passion. Not only will this be fun and perhaps help you find a career, it will enhance your college application. Keep a journal of your interesting experiences and insights. This will be useful in your college essay.

✓ Warning for those likely to qualify for financial aid: After the first $2,200 you earn each year, most colleges will reduce your financial aid by 50 cents for every dollar you earn. Consider that when deciding between a high-paying job or a meaningful low- or no-pay experience.

✓ Start work on your college admission essays. *The Fiske Guide to Colleges* lists recent essay topics for 300+ colleges.

✓ Talk with college students who are home on vacation.

✓ Decide how much to prepare for the SAT I (or ACT). Get a test prep book or computer program. Take one of its mock exams under timed conditions. If your score isn't high enough for your target colleges, use the book or program to study.

✓ Call the college admissions office for admission and financial aid materials. Request an early estimate of financial aid.

Senior Year of High School

SEPTEMBER

✓ If you haven't already taken the SAT I or ACT, register for the October administration. The registration deadline is in early September.

✓ Keep your grades up. For many colleges, this is the most important semester.

✓ If you haven't already done so, use the techniques in Chapter 2 to narrow your list of colleges.

✓ If you expect to perform or play a varsity sport in college, have your coach contact the coaches at prospective colleges.

✓ If applying Early Decision or Early Action, give recommendation forms and your résumé to your recommenders.

OCTOBER

✓ Take the SAT I or ACT.

✓ Make copies of applications and start filling them out. You can often save lots of time by using a special application such as the Common Application (*www.comonapp.org*), which allows you to apply to as many as you like of hundreds of colleges with one basic application.

✓ If you're applying Early Decision or Early Action, the deadline is coming up.

✓ Give recommendation forms and your résumé to your recommenders.

✓ Work on your essay(s).

✓ Check with each college to find out which financial aid form(s) are required and the deadlines for filing.

NOVEMBER

✓ Only if you think your score will increase *at least* 60 points (for example, you freaked out or were sick on your first exam) *and* your previous SAT I or ACT score is 60 to 150 points too low for your target colleges, register to retake the SAT I in December.

✓ Remind recommenders of deadlines.

✓ Work on applications. Most deadlines for college applications aren't until later, but check to be sure!

DECEMBER

✓ Send off your applications before the deadline. If you're an athlete or performer, be sure to send a demo tape.

✓ Request transcripts to be sent to colleges requiring them.

✓ Talk with local graduates of colleges you're considering.

✓ During vacation, complete any unfinished applications.

JANUARY/FEBRUARY

✓ Even if your family is well-off, apply for financial aid so you can be considered for merit-based scholarships. A must: Submit financial aid forms by the deadlines; you needn't wait until your parents have done their tax return. Check each college's financial aid materials for specifics.

✓ If you think you'd interview well, request an interview at private colleges or with a local alumni interviewer.

✓ If your colleges require it, have your midyear grade transcripts sent.

SPRING

✓ Use the tips in Chapter 1 to figure out the colleges at which you are most likely to be happy and successful.

✓ Application deadlines for many Canadian universities are in May and June.

✓ Consider doing something nonacademic but substantive for a semester or a year before starting college (see pp. 37–39). Most colleges will let you do this. Just convince your college that you're taking the time off to do something substantial, not just sleep late.

✓ If you're unhappy with being wait-listed, with a financial aid award, or with a housing assignment, consider an appeal.

✓ Tell all the colleges that offered you admission where you've decided to enroll. Send in your housing form as soon as possible. Early birds often get the best housing. Latecomers may not get housing at all.

✓ Submit a final transcript to the college you've selected.

✓ Consider taking Advanced Placement exams.

✓ June 30, or your last day of high school enrollment, whichever comes first, is the deadline for submitting your SAR (Federal Financial Aid report) to your college's financial aid office.

✓ Be proud. You've completed a tough task!

SUMMER

✓ Develop or explore a passion. It may give you a greater sense of purpose as you begin college.

✓ Develop your game plan for making the most of the college you've selected. (See Chapter 5.)

✓ Pack for college. (Don't forget the items on pp. 86–89.)

✓ Leave home for your new home. Be your best self and have fun.

✓ Write to thank me or blame me. I'd really appreciate suggestions for how to improve this book.

Marty Nemko

Mnemko@well.com

or

5936 Chabolyn Terrace

Oakland, CA 94618

APPENDIX D
Application Deadline Form

College applications have more deadlines than a journalist. This will help you keep track. Write in each deadline. Check weekly to see which ones are coming up. Each time you meet one, cross it out.

	COLLEGE 1	COLLEGE 2	COLLEGE 3	COLLEGE 4	COLLEGE 5	COLLEGE 6	COLLEGE 7	COLLEGE 8
Your deadline for submitting the application (Regular Action or Early Decision/Action/Admission)								
Last date you can take SAT I or ACT								
Last date you can take SAT II								
Deadline for submitting Advanced Placement test scores								
Deadline for submitting your transcript								
Deadline for submitting your mid-senior-year transcript								
Deadline for submitting your recommendations								
Deadline for filing the FAFSA								
Deadline for filing the Profile								
Deadline for filing any other required financial aid forms								
Deadline for informing colleges whether you'll attend								
Deadline for sending final transcript to your college								
Deadline for submitting AP test scores								

APPENDIX E
How to Find a Cool Career

Why choose a career this early in your life? Having a tentative career choice may help you select your major wisely. Know your major and you can make sure that each college you apply to has a strong program in that major. And remember, you aren't chained to your choice of major or career. You can always change.

Having a tentative career means you can select classes, term-paper topics, fieldwork assignments, and summer activities that will help prepare you to be a star in your career. Those things stand out on your résumé and scream, "This job applicant is great!"

Five Steps to a Cool Career

1. **Figure out what skills you enjoy using:**

    a. Make a list of everything you ever worked on that was fun and successful, starting back when you were a little kid, everything from fixing your two-wheeler to fixing the errors in your lab experiment. Especially think of projects that were so absorbing, you lost track of time.

    b. For each of these accomplishments, write the main skills you used.

    c. Look over your list of skills. In your career, you may want to use skills that appear frequently. See if you have a core skill—the one thing you do best and enjoy most.

2. **Fantasize.** For now, imagine that you couldn't fail. How could you use your core skills in a dream career?

    If you'd like to learn about more career options, go to the career center at your high school, a nearby college, or the unemployment office. Read about careers in books like the *Occupational Outlook Handbook,* which provides a good introduction to 250 popular careers or my book, *Cool Careers for Dummies,* which provides introductions to 512 great careers that most people would never have thought of. Or sit down with one of the computerized career programs found at most colleges' career centers such as Discover, Eureka, or Sigi Plus. You'll get a list of possible good-fit careers. Pick one or more that sound intriguing.

A suggestion you may hate: If your parent likes his or her career, consider a similar one. I know this is the opposite of what most people will tell you. They'll say, "Be your own person. Don't let your parents influence you." But there are reasons to consider your parent's career. Genetically, you are similar to your parents, your upbringing is probably similar, they may have taught you secrets about their career that an outsider would never get to hear, they can give you inside advice on how to prepare for that career and leads to good jobs, and they can offer counsel when you're in the career.

3. **Meet with a few people in the careers you're interested in.** Most people like to talk about their careers. Sometimes, all you need to do is pick a few names out of the Yellow Pages, call and say, "This is Joe Jones. I'm a high school student who is thinking about becoming an X, and wonder if you might be willing to tell me a little about what you do?" Call a few people and at least one is bound to say yes. Ask how she got into the career, what a typical day is like, what skills are key, what's the best way to prepare for the career, who else should you talk with, and what should you read?

4. **In light of steps 1 to 3 above, what's your dream career?** Think big! There's an old saying, "Think big, believe big, act big, and the results will be big."

5. **Think hard and talk with folks about how you could make your dream job come true.** Volunteer to work alongside a star in your desired field? A term paper on a career-related topic? A summer job? An internship? Go directly to the person who could hire you?

APPENDIX F
How to Choose a Good-Fit Major

One student said that she wanted to major in mortuary science because she likes to work with people. You can pick more wisely.

Many people think you should wait to choose a major until you're in college. That's often bad advice! Why? If you choose now, you can find a college with a good program in that major. Also, having a major will mean you have a "home" when you arrive on campus—an advisor in that department and a club for students in that major. Besides, if you choose your major carefully, you may avoid having to change majors three times and the ever more popular six-year graduation plan.

A Wise Choice of Major in Four Steps

1. Research the options. Here's how.

   ✓ Scan descriptions of each of 600 majors in the *Index of Majors and Graduate Degrees.* (The College Board, revised annually.) I know that 600 sounds like a lot of majors to read about, but each is described in 25 words or less—a total of only 30 pages—so within an hour, you'll probably have discovered lots of options you've probably never considered. Ever think of majoring in acupuncture, enology (winemaking), virology (viruses), recreational therapy, playwriting, oceanography, museum studies, gerontology (aging), forensics (how to analyze criminal evidence)? Don't like those? The *Index of Majors and Graduate Degrees* contains 591 more. *Profiles of American Colleges* (Barron's, revised annually) also contains an Index of College Majors that includes 580 majors and describes 100 of the more popular ones.

   ✓ Take a pencil-and-paper or computerized majors inventory such as *Major-Minor Finder* or the *Educational Interest Inventory.* They're available at many high schools' counseling offices.

   ✓ Learn what you can do with various careers at *www.uncwil.edu/stuaff/career/majors.htm*

2. **In light of step 1 and your tentative career, select one or two majors.** If you know you'll go to graduate school soon after college (70 percent say they will, but only 20 percent actually do), it isn't as important that you choose a career-related major; you can do that in graduate school. If you suspect that you might not go to graduate school, consider a career-related major such as engineering, business, nursing, or teacher education, or at least take some career-related courses.

3. **Find out which of the 10 to 15 colleges on your prospect list (see p. 10) offer that major and read about that major in a college catalog.**

4. **In your first term at college, take the introductory course in your prospective major.** WARNING: Don't let one course sway you too much. The rest of the major could be quite different.

APPENDIX G
Do You Want to Play a Varsity Sport?

Why play on the varsity? I'll tell you why I did, even though in four years, I actually got to play a total of about six minutes. It felt like an honor to represent my college, I enjoyed traveling to other schools, being part of a team, having people watch me play (or watch me sit on the bench), and getting coached to improve my skills. Besides, it's fun to play a sport. Even putting on the uniform felt great.

But know this: Only 2 percent of high school football and basketball players receive scholarships to play in college, and most of those are partial scholarships. And here's something even more important—if you think you're going to make the pros, here's the rule: Unless you were a high school All-American, you have a better chance of being bitten by a rattlesnake while you're in bed than of making it into the pros.

The downside of playing on the varsity? Even in Division III or NAIA, playing on the varsity usually means 20+ hours a week. It's hard to squeeze in time for studying, a social life, and a part-time job.

Your high school coach can probably tell you how likely you are to play for the college varsity, and at what level Division I, II, III, NAIA, club, or intramural, or with your 10-year-old cousin. Rule of thumb: Assuming you were on an average high school team in an average league, if you were in the top one-third of players, you'll probably be able to play varsity college ball at least in Division III or NAIA.

APPENDIX H
Sure You Want to Go Straight to College?

A question you may not want to think about: **Are you sure you want to go straight from high school to college?** Next to a home, college is the biggest purchase most families ever make. And it's an expense that requires four to six years of your time, not to mention years of paying back loans.

Today, college is too often viewed as a magic pill, the solution to every clueless high school senior's problem. So you need to make sure that you're going to college because it's right for you, not because of the hype.

Here are three students who aren't sure they want to go straight to college, and what your college coach has to say to them.

Student #1: "I'm not much of a student. I mainly get Cs and only got an 850 on the SAT I (17 on the ACT). But almost everyone's going to college and my parents are pushing me to go. Should I?"

If college *prep* courses have been a struggle, actual four-year college courses may be overwhelming. Fewer than one in five college students with your high school grades and test scores ever graduate. Now, the good news. Even without a two-year degree, you needn't be stuck with a McJob. Many good career and life paths *don't* require a college degree. These days, you can launch a successful career by apprenticing with a World Wide Webmaster, learning how to repair high-tech equipment in the military, or taking a resort management program via a short, nondegree program at a community college. (Can you picture yourself in Hawaii?) For more information on un-college options, visit your high school's career center or counselor, or ask your family and friends about their jobs. Interested in an apprenticeship? Look in the government section in the front of your nearest big-city White Pages and you'll find a listing for a local, state, or federal agency in charge of apprenticeships.

Student #2: "I'm smart enough for college, but I'm sick of school. If I go to college, I just might goof off, especially because my parents won't be there to bug me."

To keep your options open, apply to colleges. While you're waiting to hear from them, plan a time-out year to do something real-world before starting college. For example, how about working in a hospital? Apprenticing with a master guitarmaker? Teaching an illiterate adult to read? Or all of these. (For more time-out ideas, see pp. 37–39.)

When you're accepted to a college, you can either say that you'll enroll right away or ask the college to hold your place for a semester or even a year. Most colleges will say yes.

Student #3: "I could do fine at college, but I'd rather start my own business or try to get a decent job."

Today, many people think you're a loser if you don't go to college. College is a must for most good students, but not for all. Don't fall for the line, "People who go to college earn more money than those who don't." They do make more money, but college isn't the main reason. College-bound students, on average, are more able and motivated than other students. So, even if the college-bound people never actually went to college and were locked in a closet for the four years, they'd probably end up, on average, earning more money.

Especially if they're brilliant, persistent, or have family connections, some people do succeed without a college degree, for example: seven U.S. presidents from George Washington to Harry Truman, Domino's Pizza founder Tom Monaghan, Bill Gates, Quentin Tarantino (Director of *Pulp Fiction*), Tony Robbins (success guru and consultant to the Clintons), Barbra Streisand, ABC-TV's Peter Jennings, Wendy's founder Dave Thomas, Thomas Edison, Blockbuster Video president Wayne Huizenga, Ernest Hemingway, McDonald's founder Ray Kroc, Henry Ford, Helena Rubenstein, Walt Disney,

Ben Franklin, Alexander Graham Bell, John D. Rockefeller, Malcolm X, Apple Computer founder Steve Jobs, and thousands of other computer whizzes.

These folks did their learning at what I call *You U.,* by reading books, taking one-day seminars and individual courses, apprenticing with talented people, learning a lot on the job, and today, learning a lot on the Internet. If you're confident that you can succeed without college, you will avoid four to six years of school, save your family tons of money, and get a big head start on your career. You may even learn much more because you've crafted a completely individualized program, filled with hands-on learning and teachers that you've hand-picked from a variety of schools and workplaces. Many students graduate from college and lament that they remember very little of what they learned in their classes.

But before chucking college, hold on. The un-college option is a risky one. Many employers insist on a bachelor's degree. Also, more and more jobs require high-level math and science skills, which may be easier to acquire in college than on your own. Before deciding not to apply to college, talk with people in the fields you find exciting and see what opportunities exist without college. You don't want to end up in a career in which the most intelligent question you ever ask is, "Paper or plastic?"

And remember one very important thing. College is not just for career preparation, it's for—pardon my sounding like a parent—life preparation. (And, of course, for meeting fabulous men or women.) College usually improves your writing, speaking, and thinking skills, increases your knowledge and appreciation of the arts and sciences, and, in general, makes you a more thoughtful human being.

In sum, if you can handle the work, you probably should go to college. But don't get caught up in the everyone-goes-to-college fad. Choose college only if it's right for you.

INDEX

ABOUT THE AUTHOR

Marty Nemko is among the nation's most prominent college and career counselors. In addition to advising over 1,000 college-bound students and their families, he has appeared on hundreds of radio and TV shows, including nationwide on CBS, CNN, and PBS. He has been a consultant to the Educational Testing Service, ACT, and *Consumer Reports.* His column appears every Sunday in the employment sections of the *Los Angeles Times* and the *San Francisco Examiner/Chronicle.* His previous books include *How to Get an Ivy League Education at a State University, How to Get Your Child a Private School Education in a Public School,* and *Cool Careers for Dummies,* which is the #2 best-selling career guide in the nation. He holds a Ph.D. in education from the University of California, Berkeley. KCBS Radio called him "The Ralph Nader of Education." Marty Nemko and his associate offer college and career counseling, both by phone and in person. Reach them at *mnemko@well.com* or 510-655-2777.